To Love a Dog

The Story of One Man, One Dog, and a Lifetime of Love and Mystery

Tom Inglis

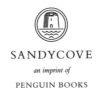

SANDYCOVE

an imprint of

PENGUIN BOOKS

SANDYCOVE

UK | USA | Canada | Ireland | Australia
India | New Zealand | South Africa

Sandycove is part of the Penguin Random House group of companies
whose addresses can be found at global.penguinrandomhouse.com.

First published 2020
001
Copyright © Tom Inglis, 2020

Set in 13.5/17.75 pt Perpetua Std
Typeset by Integra Software Services Pvt. Ltd, Pondicherry
Printed and bound in Great Britain by Clays Ltd, Elcograf S.p.A.

A CIP catalogue record for this book is available from the British Library

ISBN: 978-1-844-88491-9

www.greenpenguin.co.uk

Penguin Random House is committed to a
sustainable future for our business, our readers
and our planet. This book is made from Forest
Stewardship Council® certified paper.

To Love a Dog

Tom Inglis is a sociologist and a lifelong dog lover. Born and raised in Dublin, he now lives in a former schoolhouse (the school was once attended by John McGahern) in County Roscommon. For eighteen years he lived alongside Pepe, his beloved Wheaten terrier bitch. He is the author of several books, including *Making Love: A Memoir* and *Moral Monopoly: The Rise and Fall of the Catholic Church in Modern Ireland*.

For Olwen

Early Signs

We did not get out much yesterday, so in the evening, although it was pitch dark, I suggested a walk down to the lake. It was a bit stupid, as the path had become very overgrown and, in the darkness, could be found only through memory. The thick grass was wet and slippery. I could see the edge of the lake in the distance. It was just a case of getting there through the array of holes, hidden stones and clumps of weeds. It didn't help that I had had a couple of glasses of wine. In the past, I could have relied on her. But not now: she was far too old and far too deaf and blind.

As we stumbled along the little headland that juts out into the lake, the madness of the excursion became more apparent. If I fell in, there was nothing that she could do to help me; and if she fell in, I would probably drown trying to save her.

The lake was still; the wind had died. There was a sense of us being at the edge of space and time. We stood silently. I had no idea what she was thinking. Was she resentful that, yet again, it was I who had suggested the walk? Did she feel some obligation? She has learned that I am the source of all that is good in her life. In her magical world, I am the light. I am God. So wherever I go she must try to follow. In her world, she can never be sure what will happen next. There could be food. There could be something to chase. There could be excitement.

As we turned away from the dark beauty of the lake and started back to the lights of the house on the hill above us, she suddenly lunged to the left and was inches from falling into the lake. I screamed at her and immediately felt remorseful.

When we got back to the house, she ignored me as I sat down to watch television. But then, many minutes later, she came over and looked at me. It was a warm look of wonderment, as if she understood that we were both helpless creatures caught in time. We were both a collection of atoms flying through time and space that had become attached to each other.

And then she came closer and slowly put her head on my lap. I stroked her and we stayed like that for some minutes, and then she upped and walked away back to her bed, where she sat and watched me. I wondered what was going through her mind.

When it was time for me to go to bed, I left the door to the bedroom upstairs open. It was an invitation for her to come upstairs to the other bed she has there. The bedroom is her daytime refuge. As I sat in bed reading, I kept listening out for the sounds of her coming up. But there was nothing. I turned out the lights and then, in the dark silence, I heard her coming. I lay still and she came into the room. She stopped for a while and then turned around and walked out back downstairs. Was she being deliberately cold? Maybe I had let her down. Maybe I was selfish. Maybe I had pushed her too far.

But there was another deeper, darker thought. Mixed with feelings of sympathy and concern there was a growing realisation that, someday soon, I was going to have to arrange her death.

The Lakehouse

Pepe and I have been together for seventeen years. Despite the male name, which I will explain later, she is female. We have walked many roads together, explored paths through woods and trekked across mountains.

Last night's escapade seems to have had no effect on her. This morning she bounced up the stairs into the bedroom full of joy, alert, ready for action, tail erect and quivering. She came to the bed and all I could do was put out my hands and hold her head and stroke her. I told her that I would be lost without her. She made no response, but I think she understood the tone of my voice.

Pepe doesn't do moods, doesn't bear grudges. She has a memory, of course, but it is not like my memory. It is as if she only has good memories. I like it that when she sees me, she cannot help but be happy. Wouldn't it be great if humans could be like that? Imagine not playing the game of hurt and resentment. Imagine meeting those we love, those to whom we are attached, and feeling helplessly happy, wagging our bums from side to side.

She is becoming deafer by the day. Not so long ago, she used to hang on my every word, particularly in the early morning or after dinner. I would say something like: 'Is there a dog in the room that would like to go for a walk in the not too distant future?' I'd say it quickly, but she would understand and jump up in anticipation. Now I have to ask her slowly, saying the word 'walk' loud and clear.

We live in an old schoolhouse. The previous owners bought it from the Catholic Church at the beginning of the 1970s and used it as a holiday home.

When I came to buy what I now call 'The Lakehouse' in 2015, there was a delay in closing the purchase: it was still registered as a schoolhouse. The design was simple: two big rooms, each with its own door. By the time my neighbour Anne attended the school, in the late 1960s, there was only a single teacher and just one of the rooms was used as a classroom.

The writer John McGahern attended the school. McGahern began life on a small farm near Ballinamore, twenty miles away. But after his mother died, his father, who was the Garda sergeant in Cootehall, brought him and his siblings to live in the barracks here in Cootehall. The old schoolhouse is about a mile from the village of Cootehall, and as I look across the lake I can imagine John and his siblings walking the road out of the village and up and down Fox Hill, which overlooks Lake Drumharlow and the surrounding country-side. McGahern describes the walk home from the school in his short story 'Coming into His Kingdom': the tranquillity of the road mixed with the laughter and teasing of young girls and boys.

The Irish countryside is dotted with abandoned two-room schoolhouses, relics of the time when more than half the population of Ireland lived in rural areas. Like most of these buildings, my schoolhouse is within spitting distance of the road. Traffic and parking were not concerns in the decades when it was open. Nor were health and safety: the school-house is on a bad bend on the road, and the field behind leads down to the lake. There are hundreds of lakes in this part of Ireland. Most of them are small and self-contained. Lake Drumharlow is different. It connects to the River Boyle, which flows into the River Shannon, which in turn flows into the Atlantic.

Cootehall today is very different from the village that McGahern described in his writings. In those days, there were three pubs and three shops. Now there is just one pub and no shops. Like many other villages, Cootehall is dom-inated, physically and symbolically, by an enormous Catholic church. Like the pub opposite, it is struggling to stay alive.

The road on which I live goes from Cootehall into Carrick-on-Shannon: the nearest town. It is a narrow country road bordered for the most part by thick hedgerows. It is full of twists and turns, dips and little hills. In many parts, it is so narrow that there is not enough room for two cars to pass.

During the day, except for some tractors and vans, the road is quiet. But in the morning and evening, there are commuters, mainly workers, parents and schoolchildren, coming from and going to Carrick-on-Shannon.

I can open the front door of the Lakehouse and step directly into the beauty of nature. It is overwhelming and, for me, still very new. Until I bought the Lakehouse, I had never lived in the country. Both of my grandparents were Dubliners. I had no country cousins. I never stayed, let alone lived, on a farm. I had no relatives or friends who came from a farming background. For years I taught sociology in University College Dublin, and never knew much about life in rural Ireland. Even now, after two years, I still can't tell a heifer from a bullock.

The Morning Walk

Pepe always does her poo within the first hundred yards of leaving the house. She squats on the grass verge at the side of the road. There are times and places when it is important to pick up her poo – I am a dab hand with the plastic bag – but this is not one of them.

After she has done her business, she will often bound down the road, full of joy in anticipation of the walk ahead. She may be quite deaf and blind, but she is obedient enough that I can walk with her off the lead. I have never liked her being on a lead when it is not necessary. Most of the time when I see dogs on leads they are out in front, choking themselves, gasping for air, pulling their masters behind them. It is a strange image. Dogs have to be controlled, but well-trained dogs can be controlled by the voice of their owners.

Pepe is a dog. She is not human. She is not a child. She is not a cuddly teddy bear. I believe that dogs should be able to mooch, sniff and squirt with as much freedom as possible. I know that dogs can scare people, particularly young children, or adults who have had bad experiences. And I know from cycling the roads of Ireland that an uncontrolled dog can be dangerous. There is nothing worse than a mad cur charging out of a house and snapping at my feet as I try desperately to pedal my way to safety. Indeed there have been a few times when I have ended up in the ditch.

Although in the past Pepe always responded immediately to my voice and whistle, now there is the fear that, because of her deafness, she will not hear me. So, increasingly, I have to stay beside her as she does her poo and be ready to shout at her if she begins to run away.

From the schoolhouse, the road leads down to the corner of the lake. There are signs of spring. The reeds on the lakeside, which died down over the winter, are beginning to reappear. The small white buds of the hawthorn bushes are about to flourish. There are dandelions, daisies and primroses. It is still early morning. The sun is rising, its rays breaking through the clouds, making the ripples on the lake sparkle. I can feel the tingle. It is my early-morning shower of beauty.

At the corner of the lake, there is a bridge under which a small stream runs into the lake. To the right, there is a lane that goes up to a bog. It is a cul-de-sac with no traffic except on those mornings when Kieran, a local farmer, drives up in his van to check on and feed his cattle before going to work. The land around here is not good. It is thick and clumpy and full of wiry grasses and rushes. Most farmers need some other form of employment to survive.

The lane is a narrow corridor bordered on either side by thickets of willow, briars, ferns and grasses and, in summer, bunches of pink and white flowers, loosestrife, fireweed and honeysuckle. The hedgerows form a cordon of thick, wide growth so dense that there is no possibility of Pepe, or me, getting into the fields that border it. A ridge of grass, mixed with dandelions and daisies, has grown up and runs along the middle of the black tarmacked road.

For a dog brought up on the streets of Dublin, the countryside must seem unexciting at times. There are no lampposts or signposts, or gates covered with the pee of those who have walked before her. Occasionally, a woman from a nearby townland drives over to the start of the lane and walks her dog from there down to the bog. But this happens only in the afternoon, and mostly in summer.

So Pepe has to make do with the scent of flowers mixed occasionally with the smell of a cat, mink, stoat, weasel, fox, badger or pine marten. When she comes upon one of these, she can get lost in it for minutes. She is intoxicated. But these are not everyday delights, and I suspect she would prefer to be back in Dublin, with a steady supply of fresh dog pee and poo to sniff.

I let the thoughts of the day drift in and out as we head towards the rising sun. We pass Martin's house up on a small incline to our right and then wind our way round a bend to the small bungalow in which he grew up. Like many houses in remote areas around here, it is derelict. In the summer months, the small garden that surrounds the house is an occasional home to some cattle.

The lane then straightens for about two hundred yards. At the end of this stretch there is another small incline up to a bunch of fir trees. Kieran's cow shed is on the right. Reaching the shed is a reminder for me to look back down the lane for Pepe. She is a thing of beauty in the distance, running towards me at full tilt, her mouth open, her ears pinned back, her eyes glistening in the sun. I like to think that she is smiling. She is certainly happy. In those moments she reminds me of the intense, fleeting joy of being alive. No thoughts, no worries, just pure being.

I squat down to welcome her. She is not the sort of dog who will run into my arms, tail wagging furiously, and cover my hands and face in slobbery licks. She does not do affection that way. She stops beside me, but only for a second. She is too busy. There is no thought in her head of stopping to share this moment of love and beauty. There is no time. There is still too much to be explored. In this moment, she seems so young.

From Kieran's shed the lane descends gradually down to the bog, making a couple of small swerves between thickets of ferns until it reaches two large steel gates. The gate on the left goes up to Declan's farm. Declan, another part-time farmer, also works for Shane, the builder who did the renovations on the Lakehouse. The other gate leads into the bog. I tried walking through it a couple of times, but it is a minefield of muddy holes, some of which are quite deep. The last time we tried it, Pepe fell into one. It meant a shower when we got home, something she hates.

The gates, then, are the signal that we have reached the end of the road and it is time to turn back. Again I squat and wait for her to come to me. This is the time and place where I demand my moment of affection. She knows the routine. She stops about ten yards away before walking slowly towards me, a reluctant lover. I pet her head and rub my hand along her back. She wags her tail perfunctorily. After a minute, maybe even less, she becomes unsettled. She is anxious to get going. She is anticipating her breakfast, her one and only meal of the day. It has been the same for years: a tin of dog food in the morning and a few biscuits in the evening. I am convinced that this restricted diet has been central to keeping her alive for so long. But as her life nears its end, I am beginning to let the regime go and give her little treats.

On the return back down the lane, I have to be careful. It is hard to constrain her excitement. In the twinkle of an eye, she can take off and run away home at full speed. It seems that once she gets the thought of food into her head, no amount of shouting will stop her. Up to recently, she always stopped when she came to the main road. However, in the past month or so, she regularly charges out of the lane and up the road towards the house. In the morning, during commuter hour, there are often cars hurtling around the bend at the bridge. I run behind her as fast as I can, panting and praying for no car to come and saying to myself that this is the end: I will have to put her on the lead from now on.

Carried Away

We drove into Carrick today. Since she was a pup, Pepe has liked going for a drive as much as a walk. In the early years, she would sit on the front seat, pushing her nose out over the edge of the wound-down window, letting the wind blow over her face. When she'd had enough, she would come back in and sit upright on the seat, looking out at the road ahead. Driving Miss Pepe.

Sometimes, in those days when she was only getting to know me, I would suddenly shout and scream at the idiocy of some other driver, and she would jump off the seat and cower down beneath the glove compartment. It was cute and pathetic. I would apologise and try to explain that it had nothing to do with her. But she would not come back up. She was too traumatised. If I could, I would stop the car and encourage her to come back up. Sometimes she did.

My wife, Aileen, who died in 2005, did not love Pepe the way I did. She saw her more as a dog than a member of the family. This led to disagreements and, sometimes, rows. This has to be put in context. There were very few things that Aileen and I rowed about. She was a kind, warm, generous woman. She was creative, vivacious and mischievous. But she was not a doggy person. She could walk past a cute puppy without any urge to bend down and pet it. I used to cringe with disappointment when she came home from work and ignored Pepe's greeting.

Aileen grew up with dogs, but they were always kept outside. She was not used to them being in the house or in the car. These were contested sites. Aileen used to go mad when she discovered that I had let Pepe up on the front seat of her car. In a way she was right. Besides the issue of dirt and smells, Pepe's nails did damage the seat. But for me, keeping the seat pristine was nothing compared to the pleasure of driving along with the dog I loved sitting up on the seat beside me, leaning over to sniff the air through the open window.

Perhaps it's wrong to say that someone is either a doggy person or not. Perhaps it is more of a continuum. On a doggy scale of one to ten, I would say Aileen was about a three. After a few gin and tonics, she might get up to seven or even eight. After she died, I took over her car and, without any sense of guilt, I let Pepe up on the seat all the time. And yes, within a year or two, the seat was ruined. But as I used to say to anyone who winced at the thought of having to sit on the shredded seat, 'That's Pepe's seat. A car is for travelling, a dog is for life.'

I think Pepe knew that I was allowing her to be where she was not supposed to be. She knew that there was one rule for being with me and another rule when she was with Aileen. She lived in a world of fine differences, learning how to adapt her behaviour depending on whether she was with me, or Aileen, or our children Arron and Olwen.

Shortly after we set off on our journey into Carrick, she looked over towards me and, as if in appreciation, she lifted her paw and held it out to me. As in the past, I did not take it immediately. I knew the refusal to take her paw when it was first offered would provoke a response. So she leaned over towards me, moving her paw up and down, looking at me, pleading for me to respond: she wanted me to take my hand from the wheel for a moment and hold her paw. And so I did. And then she stopped and sat still, but not for long. Soon the exercise was repeated. It is a ritualised form of communication, of gestures made and received, reaching across the chasm of reason and language that separates us. This ritual always makes me melt.

Of course, I know that it is not safe to pet and drive, but I have always been careful and she seems to understand that when we come to turning a corner or changing lane, the petting has to stop. This ritual of pawing and petting can go on for five to ten minutes. Eventually she stops, curls round and round the seat a few times, and then lies down.

A Walk on the Wild Side

I know that she is going to die sooner rather than later. It is like watching the tide go out. But for the moment she is here and she is very much alive. As always, the pleasure is in watching her enjoying life, being led by her nose, surrendering to the moment, the sheer exuberance of exploring. Dogs and children are a reminder of the constraints of the adult world in which we live; a world that is rational, reasonable and controlled, but often so disenchanted and boring.

And this is what I love about her and about being with her. Just the two of us wandering down the lane, each of us lost in our own world. She belongs to the world of smells; I belong to the world of thoughts. There has always been a balance, a kind of symbiotic relationship, of needing and being aware of the other. The task for both of us is to be mindful of each other. But sometimes I get lost in my thoughts and I turn around and she is not there. Likewise, she gets lost in a smell, and when she comes to, she is so disoriented that she runs off in the wrong direction. In the past, she would quickly realise the error of her ways and stop and wait for me to come and find her. It was a trick she learned herself. To have faith in the god she trusts: that somehow, like magic, he would turn up. When I did, she would never make any gesture of thanks or apology. She would just wag her tail a little and head off into the world again.

Getting Lost

It is this ability to get lost, and not to get distressed, that impresses me most. This trust that she is safe, that she will not be attacked, and that eventually I will come and find her. And there have been many times when she has got lost and I have found her.

One morning, Olwen and I were at home together in Dublin when we realised that she was missing. She was only a puppy, and the sense of panic was immediate and intense. I imagined a scene of Pepe trundling across a road, of cars braking, and of her being squashed. We ran up and down the surrounding roads and back lanes, shouting out her name, all to no avail. She had no name tag. She was not chipped. Every time we turned a corner I braced myself for the sight of her dead body. I imagined going round the neighbourhood putting up those notices that you see taped to lampposts.

We had to expand the circles of our search. We ran back to the house to get my car and then drove towards Terenure, hoping that she had followed the route of her morning and evening walk. Then, thinking that she might have missed the turn on Brighton Road and kept on straight, we drove that way. And then we saw her, sniffing around a rubbish bin, blissfully unaware of all the anxiety she had caused.

More recently, she got lost again. I was back up in Dublin, staying with my partner, Carol. She and her daughter, Stevie, took Pepe out one evening. As they walked around the suburban roads of Churchtown, Pepe trailed along behind them. They were in a quiet estate. They crossed a road and, as usual, Carol looked back to see if Pepe had followed them. She hadn't.

After half an hour, they phoned me and I headed over to join the search. It was a dark night, already past ten o'clock. We spread the search to the surrounding area, without any luck. I was becoming disconsolate. And then, suddenly, Carol saw a woman and her daughter out walking with Pepe on a lead beside them. She was Linda Smith, the owner of the Bijou restaurant in Rathgar village. By chance she had gone to her front door and found Pepe standing there. They had taken her in and looked for a phone number on her medal, but there wasn't one. This was because, when she was young and beautiful, I had a fear of her being kidnapped and of the kidnappers demanding a ransom for her return. To overcome this, I had her name on one side of the medal and 'Chipped' on the other – I'd got her chipped after the previous disappearance. The idea was that whoever found her would take her to a police station, which would have a device for reading the data from her chip.

Linda and her daughter had decided to take Pepe for a walk before going to bed. It was then that they met Carol. Pepe recognised Carol, but not with any great enthusiasm.

She had obviously been well looked after. Not for the first time, this led to some hard questions to which I did not know the answers and which I did not really want to ask. Would Pepe have been just as happy to move in with Linda and her daughter? If Pepe had stayed with them, say, for a year, and if I then met her by chance on the street, and she recognised me, would she have left them to come back to me?

And what of Linda and her daughter? How would they feel, having become attached to Pepe, to have to give her back? I could imagine a King Solomon moment in which a neutral observer would hold the dog and Linda and I would call to her at the same time. Who would she have turned to? Probably the one to have fed her in recent times and, given that Linda owns a restaurant, I suspect I would not have had much of a chance.

In some respects it is irrelevant. I realised then that I am more attached to Pepe than she is to me. It is irrelevant how much she cares about me: I will still love her. It is one of the conditions of my existence.

Fear of Death

In 1993, Aileen created a sculpture consisting of glass flower presses, of her own design, in which she placed spring flowers that were in full bloom. The presses were about four feet high, on narrow metal legs. There were about a dozen of them. Each day, she turned the screws on the flowers. In the accompanying catalogue, she wrote:

> From the very beginning of our lives the only certainty is that we will die. Yet there is an unnatural fear of death. We are happy to look at life. We take delight in documenting its various manifestations. But we are uncomfortable looking death in the eye. We are even more uncomfortable looking at something beautiful dying. There is a time and place for death, and everything should be in its proper time and place.

A week before Aileen died, our neighbours Joanelle and Ivan brought her a bunch of tulips. After they left, she got me to put them in a vase and place them on the shelf opposite the end of the bed. As the week passed, they, like her, began to fade and droop. She was intrigued by the symbolic unity. She found the decaying flowers so mesmerising that she wanted to take photos of them. But when our son Arron took some photos, she was not happy; they did not capture the way she saw the flowers. She insisted that he lie down on the bed and get as close to her as possible to take the photos.

Now, Pepe is dying. Life is being slowly drained from her. Every few days, there are new signs of decay. I can see it in her eyes, in her movements, in her whole demeanour. There is no escape. I wonder to what extent she is aware of it.

I am afraid I will not be able to watch Pepe die. I know that it will be nothing like being with Aileen during those last months. There is not the same love, the same attachment, the same meaning. Aileen and I married young. She was twenty; I was twenty-two. We had been together since she was sixteen. We were two saplings that became enmeshed in each other.

I am afraid that watching Pepe die will open up memories of Aileen's death. Thirteen years may seem like a long time, but grief does not obey time.

We like to say that people die 'peacefully'. The word is regularly put in brackets in death notices. As Aileen said, we deny the reality of death. To overcome her own fear, she persuaded an undertaker to allow her to lie in one of his coffins.

Aileen loved life. Up to the last week, disabled as she was, she was out and about, playing cards, visiting friends, having lunch with her parents. The day before she died, she was laughing and joking with family members as if she were on her way to a party. And then, that last night, she knew it was all over, that death was coming to take her. Just after midnight, some hours before she died, having run out of things to say, I started singing 'Some Enchanted Evening' from *South Pacific*. When I finished, she started laughing and said it was unfair for me to sing our favourite song when she could not dance with me.

The memory of those last few hours with Aileen, when we finally stopped talking and laughing and she began to fight death, still haunts me. Watching death spread its fingers around her. I talked and talked, as she grimaced and gritted her teeth. And then the movements stopped. Soon there was just a series of sighs and whimpers. By then I could no longer talk. I just lay beside her, hoping that she would give in quickly.

Often when I am melancholic, I look into Pepe's eyes and she stares back into mine. I tell her softly: 'You know nothing, you dumb animal.' She listens and tilts her head to the side as if it might help her understand better. I pet her and whisper 'walk' in her ear. She reacts immediately and starts to run and jump about. There is life in the old dog yet.

A Wolf in Dog's Clothing

What, then, is this relationship I have with Pepe? How and why is it that, like millions and millions of humans throughout the ages, I have been sucked into not just looking after her, but being devoted to her? When I think of all the time and money that I have spent on her, of how much anxiety she has caused, of what an inconvenience she has been, I think I must be an idiot.

It might make sense if she served some purpose. If she were a working dog, for example a collie, she could have helped me herding sheep. If she were a Labrador, she could have retrieved the birds I shot. If she were a St Bernard, she could have found me when I got lost in the Alps.

As a terrier, she should have been good at chasing and catching mice and rats. But Pepe seems to have missed this trait in her breed. She never caught a mouse or a rat in her life. In Rathgar, mice would regularly scurry across the kitchen floor in front of her bed, but she would show no sign of seeing or hearing them. If I shouted, 'Mouse!' she would run to the patio door barking furiously, wanting to be let out to chase away a cat.

But she was a great pretender. In her prime, when we were out walking, she would go in search of a stick that she thought would be suitable for me to throw. If, when she found one, I asked, 'Is that a rat?' she would shake it vigorously from side to side, indicating to me perhaps that if she ever did catch a rat she would know how to kill it.

But Pepe, like many dogs, serves other purposes. Imagine having a companion or lover who, no matter what time of day or night you came home, was overcome with genuine excitement at the sight of you, who jumped and danced around in circles, yelping with delight. Maybe some children do this. But if an adult did it, it would be read as strange, evidence of a complete loss of self. This is what makes dogs so wonderful. They don't have any sense of self.

While, like all loving relationships, my relationship with Pepe is unique, it is part of a longer story that goes back ten or fifteen thousand years. It relates to the time when human hunters began to develop a symbiotic relationship with wolves, each helping the other to find prey.

The great leap forward among human beings was when they began to realise that, instead of hunting and gathering, it would be easier, more reliable, less dangerous and more productive to stay put and use seeds to grow the plants they needed. Later they began to understand that, instead of hunting other animals, it would be better to capture and breed them. This took place over thousands of years, during which, it seems, the relationship with wolves became even stronger.

One suspects that, for a long time, humans saw the wolves mainly as a nuisance; unwanted guests hanging around the camp. They also posed a threat, not so much to adult humans, but to their offspring, food stores and livestock. But then – perhaps as part of a process of trying to master and control their environment, perhaps out of curiosity or boredom – humans began to capture the offspring of the wolves. It would seem that, in the same way as they were beginning to experiment with growing plants from seed, they kept the most docile of the wolf cubs, and then used these to breed new cubs, again keeping the docile ones. Over generations and hundreds and thousands of years, the wolves became tamer and more biddable. Once the wolves were happy to stay put – not surprising, given that they were being fed and cared for – humans began to use them primarily for hunting and protection, and also for more specific purposes we associate with different breeds of dog.

It would seem that these domesticated dogs became objects of affection and attachment. Unlike sheep, goats, pigs and horses, they looked humans in the eye. The ability to become a love object was an enormous achievement. It seems that there were three crucial elements to this. The first was being able to look humans in the eye, the second was to adapt to their ways of being, and the third was to be affectionate. As all doggy people recognise, the slow lick of a dog's tongue can release thousands of endorphins.

A Trip to the Sea

I keep on failing to recognise how disabled Pepe is by her deafness and blindness. This morning, I called her to go for a walk. After numerous attempts, she eventually heard me. It must have been like hearing a vague call of a trumpet across some desert. She arose from her bed and came running out of the living room, alert, full of life, tail held high, charging towards me. I held the door open for her, but she got it all wrong. Instead of going to the right, where the door was open, she veered to the left and went crashing into the gap between the door and the wall.

There was no yelping or crying, no anger or frustration. No shouting or screaming at me. Just confusion that the opening was not where she expected it to be. She raised herself, stood still. I had to drag her back into the hall and pull and push her out the open door.

There was a time, not so long ago, when, down in the park, I would throw a tennis ball high into the air. She would charge after it, waiting for it to bounce, and then, timing her run, she would leap into the air and catch it at the height of its arc. Sometimes, she would twist a little just as she caught it: perhaps a deliberate flourish to attract attention. Now if

I throw a ball, it sails over her head and she stares vacantly at me, thinking that I still have it. The first few times this happened, I went to fetch the ball myself. Then I gave up. Worse still: when I take a dog biscuit from the drawer in the kitchen, show it to her, and then throw it into the living room, she has no idea where it has gone. Fortunately, her sense of smell is still quite strong and she is able to sniff it out.

Yesterday evening, Carol and I took her for a walk along the headland at Streedagh, north of Sligo town. It was getting late, and the sun was beginning to descend through the clouds into the sea. The landscape there is dominated by Ben Bulben. Across the expanse of Donegal Bay there is a glimpse of Slieve League rising above the grey clouds.

We were with our friends Charles and Vivienne. Although I cannot ever remember them having a dog, they are easily classified as doggy people. They are always minding other people's dogs, including Pepe. Maybe it is a sense of duty that comes with living in a cottage that used to belong to the Master of the Hounds of Lissadell estate.

Since we had not met them for a couple of months, we immediately became engrossed in conversation. We crossed the rocky beach and began to clamber up to the headland. In the past, Pepe would have scampered up in front of us and stood at the top looking back down, as if wondering what was keeping the humans.

But those days are gone, and this time, instead of following us up the meandering path to the top, she decided to go straight up the steeper trail. She began to struggle. She tried to dig into the ground with her nails, but it gave way. She tumbled back down to the beach. I found her dazed but seemingly unhurt, and delighted to see me. I put her on the lead.

There were no sheep on the headland, so after a time I let her free. She bounded across the heath. Now and then she stumbled into a bog hole or pool of water, only to come out, shake herself down and continue on.

The descent on the far side of the headland presented another challenge. There were long lines of black rocks. The tide had turned only a couple of hours earlier. The rocks were wet and slippery, often covered in thick, slimy seaweed. It was difficult for us full-sighted humans to pick a good path.

The light was beginning to fade. In concentrating on picking out my own path across the rocks, I forgot about Pepe. When I looked back, she was quite far behind, trying to find a path, getting befuddled and going off in the wrong direction. She had lost sight of us, and she could not smell us. I called out to her. She heard me but, with the wind, could not tell from which direction I was calling.

She panicked. I ran back towards her, stumbling over the rocks. Fortunately, she stopped and I caught up with her. I apologised. I put her on the lead, but it was too short to reach to the bottom of each outcrop of rock. I let her free again and tried to keep her close to me. A couple of times she arrived at the top of a rock and looked over the edge, stopped and gazed into the abyss. She tried to inch her way down, gripping the wet rock with her nails. It was pitiful and she ended up sliding and falling to the bottom with her legs splayed out in front of her.

All the time, her tail was erect and quivering with excitement. When I stopped occasionally to pet her, she wagged her tail and pulled away, anxious to get on with the adventure. Maybe she thought it was some kind of magical play ride in doggy Disneyland.

I try to imagine what would have happened if it had been me. Old, doddery, almost deaf and blind, trying desperately to keep up with my grandchildren as they laughed and joked while they scampered across the rocks. Would I, full of bumps and bruises, jump and shout for joy and say it was great fun?

We are unable to live in the moment. We live in fear of ill health, injury and death. We are unable to live in nature. We cannot let the wild inside. Children cannot wander into the world. They are chastised if they roam beyond the supervisory eyes of their parents. They must be protected from nature.

To Pee or Not to Pee

The first time she lost control of her bladder, she came over and stood beside me when I was sitting at my desk in the study. I looked down to give her a reassuring pet of recognition and noticed that she was squatting and peeing. Was this a cry for help? It had been lashing rain since her morning walk had finished at ten. It was now four in the afternoon. She had not asked to be let out.

The next day, I came across a pool of urine on the floor in the living room. I took her to the vet. She said it could be old age but was probably just an infection. She put her on antibiotics. I thought it was all finished until two weeks later, when Pepe came over to me in the house and squatted and peed.

The vet said that her increasing blindness was mostly due to cataracts. These, she said, could be removed, but it would be costly: I would have to bring her to a special-ist. It could cost a couple of thousand. But even if I was willing to pay, the vet thought that it would be too trau-matic for her. Pepe would probably have to be in the clinic for a couple of days. The operation would be demanding and afterwards she would have to wear a special collar to prevent her scratching.

Watching Pepe deal with her blindness gives me some insight into the difficulties and frustrations she must feel when she wants to pee. She is dependent on me to let her out. And even when she is let out, it is often into the cold pitch-black of night. She has to sniff and, perhaps relying on memory, feel her way across the patio and down the steps to the garden. Sometimes she cannot find the steps and, being in desperate need to let go, pees on the patio. Other times she gets the steps wrong and stumbles into the garden. But there is never any sign of resentment or distress. She does not look for sympathy. She comes back, wagging her tail.

What is It?

Often, when I am out walking with her, doggy people will stop and, after admiring her, ask, 'What is it?' It is a bit like botanists being intrigued by a plant. I take delight in announcing that she is an Irish soft-coated wheaten terrier (ISCWT). This is one of nine native Irish breeds, the others being the Irish wolfhound, the Kerry Blue, the Irish red setter, the Irish red-and-white setter, the Irish water spaniel, the Kerry beagle, the Irish terrier, and the Glen of Imaal terrier. Pepe can be seen as belonging to a form of Irish dog aristocracy.

As my friend David Blake Knox reveals in his book on Irish dogs, the whole business of classifying and defining what constitutes a particular breed is, given the long history of dogs, relatively recent. It did not take off until the latter half of the nineteenth century. And it was not until the 1930s that the ISCWT began to be recognised as a distinct breed. The reason for the inclusion of the descriptor 'soft-coated' was that there were many terriers that could be described as wheaten by their colour. What makes the ISCWT different is that, while many terriers have double coats to protect them from harsh weather conditions, it has a wavy single coat that covers its entire body and head and that can appear to flow as the dog moves.

David shines a good light into the curious world of dog-breeding. It turns out that the mythical Irish wolfhound, the 'national' Irish dog, has little or no connection to the hounds that the legendary Fionn mac Cumhaill kept back in the days of Na Fianna. In reality, like all breeds of dog, the Irish wolfhound started out as a mongrel. Its 'look' was a concept dreamed up by an English army captain who used the various breeds then available to him to create the distinctive features that we recognise today. As with other breeds, it was a concoction. Still, the wolfhound is trooped out on state occasions as if to affirm that the Irish people, like the wolfhound, are purebreds descended from the same ancestors over thousands of years. The reality is that the Irish are a nation of half-breeds and mongrels.

Welcoming the Outsider

One of the lovely myths about the Irish, one that I think we try to live up to, is that we are an island of a thousand welcomes. In the past, this was mainly to do with bringing in tourists. More recently, it has been to do with welcoming immigrants who have come to live and work here. A generation or so ago, the Republic of Ireland was almost completely white, English-speaking and Catholic. Now one in six people living here was born elsewhere in the world.

Some people are always ready to welcome a dog that is looking for a good home. My friend Donal is a doggy person. He is devoted to Duckie, a large, wiry-haired black-and-white mongrel, about the size of an Irish setter. She has a lovely soft face. Her mouth is rounded with white hair. There is a touch of collie and perhaps whippet.

Duckie was about a year old when Donal took her on. He did so even though the staff at the dog pound felt that she might be a handful, as they believed she had been mistreated by her previous owner. Whatever the cause, she was very confused about humans. She would bound towards strangers with great optimism, as if she wanted to trust them, and then, suddenly, at the last moment, she would turn and run away. However, with those she has come to know and trust, she will happily jump into their lap and stay there.

It would seem that the world of dog owners is divided between those who, like me, choose specific breeds and others, like Donal, who go to the local rescue centre and take home a dog who otherwise might be put down. I like the idea of rescuing a dog from death. But I am not certain if I would be willing to do it again. My first dog came from the dogs' home in Dublin. I was about nine or ten years old at the time. I was looking for the new love of my life, and I was bamboozled at the number of dogs at the dogs' home. I remember my heart going out to the decrepit elderly dogs who obviously had little hope of being chosen. As I looked, my father became a little impatient. I had to choose. I went for a young black mutt with a white streak across his chest. When I got home, I named him Darkie. (It never occurred to my parents, let alone me, back in the late 1950s in Ireland, that naming a dog Darkie could be seen as offensive.)

Darkie had very few redeeming features and was not particularly friendly. But I was devoted to him. He did not last long. I remember the day I came in from school and, when I could not find him, I went to the kitchen and my mother said simply: 'Darkie has gone.' He had been ill, but I did not think *that* ill. The vet had come and pronounced 'distemper'. It was a death sentence, and he was bundled into the car and taken away to be killed.

Being a Dog

There have been hundreds, if not thousands, of books and articles written, of stories told and programmes made, that have tried to help humans see and understand the world from the perspective of a dog. We can learn a lot from people who have studied dogs scientifically. But the reality is that there is a huge chasm between the way humans and dogs see and understand the world. As the American comedian Groucho Marx put it: 'Outside of a dog, a book is man's best friend. Inside of a dog, it's too dark to read.' And yet, like I suspect many others, I spend hours and hours trying to figure out what Pepe is thinking.

I wonder what she would say if she could speak, but of course she does not have language. Language structures my world. It gives it meaning. It enables me to master and control it and to communicate with others. When I am with Pepe, I try to understand what it must be like to be in the world without language. I try to imagine what it must be like to have such a strong sense of smell, to be led by my nose. It would be a completely different kind of existence. When I met strangers, instead of smiling and talking, I would go and sniff their privates.

I also think she has a different sense of time. She knows roughly what time of day it is from the ritual nature of everyday life. She knows from the making of cups of tea and bringing them upstairs that it is morning time, and that when I come down it is walk time. She knows that when I move from my study to sit and eat in the kitchen it is lunchtime. And because these behaviours change at the weekend – I get up later, I go shopping, I go for a cycle – she has a sense of it being Saturday or Sunday. This awareness operates mainly at the level of stimulus and response. She becomes aware of something and, as if a ping goes off in her mind, she remembers that this is the time and place that certain events occur.

Although she now sleeps most of the day, she seems to know when it comes to five or six o'clock in the afternoon. It is biscuit time. So, being up in the bedroom, she makes her way down the stairs, presents herself at the patio door, goes out, does a pee and comes back into the kitchen looking for her biscuit. But what was the stimulus that got her to get up and start to do all this? I have no idea.

And obviously she has memories: she remembers people and places. She also remembers experiences and smells. When she meets someone she liked from a long time ago, she remembers who they are, their smell and character, and, if it is a fond memory, wags her tail with excitement. But to what extent does she think of them when they are not there? Is it an extreme case of 'out of sight, out of mind'? To what extent does she think of me when I am gone? To what extent did she miss Aileen after she died? To what extent does she have a sense of history, of being able to place people and events in time? Is she able to think back about an event that happened last week or last year? I think she lives much more in the moment.

Living mainly in the present does not mean that she is not able to anticipate the future. Pepe, like most dogs, is good at causal thinking. If, in the past, X has led to Y, then she is capable of comprehending that if X occurs again, it is likely to lead to Y. Sometimes I think, when she lies beside me and is constantly looking up at me, that all she does is look for certain Xs.

When she was young, she had a great ability to read events as signs of things in the present that predicted the future. She seemed to spend her day reading and interpreting my movements. I was her reality-TV show. She became very good at reading the signs and responding to them. Indeed, she became so good at this that she could read my automatic reactions better than I could. There was a way I moved in the chair that signalled I might be about to stand up. She began to understand that the chance of my getting up and going out somewhere – to the kitchen, to the garden, or better still to the park – increased when I was interrupted by a phone call. This led to her getting off the couch, stretching and coming up to the desk and pestering me every time the phone rang.

There is an element of anticipation and prediction and, to some extent, mastery and control in all of this. She is able to manipulate the present to create a different future. But this is different from waking up in the morning, thinking of the day ahead and plotting what will happen.

And it seems that memory and stimulus don't operate in the same way. If I say 'walk', it stimulates excitement. But I don't think there is any point in saying, as one might do to a child, 'Let's go for a walk in the wood,' as opposed to, for example, 'a walk by the sea'. A child remembers previous walks, and, having language, is able to connect the word 'wood' or 'sea' with the relevant memory. She is able to conjure up an image of what is to come. I don't think it works the same way with Pepe. When she arrives at the wood or the sea, she remembers where she is and, given past experiences, is able to predict and, to some extent, control what happens next.

As much as she does not live in the past, nor does she live in the future to anything like the same extent that humans do. Yes, she has learned from a crude system of stimulus and response that if she does something bold, there will be chastisement, or a reward if she is good. But she does not live in fear of punishment. Nor, of course, does she live in hope. This is one of the things that make her attractive. Compared to humans, she is fearless of what might happen to her and hopeless about doing anything to avoid it.

Living in the present means not being able to master and control the world. And, perhaps, the more we stop trying to master and control it, the more we try to be a species *for* the world rather than merely *in* it, the more we try to understand and appreciate the environment, the sooner we will stop destroying it. There is much to be learned from dogs and other animals. They could teach us humans some new tricks about how to live our lives.

Dog Abuse

I am lucky. I am reasonably well off. I live in a nice house in a beautiful part of Ireland. I exist in a cocoon of love made up of family and friends. Although I have suffered great loss, I have never experienced cruelty, let alone sustained and repeated violence. I have never lived in inhumane conditions. Although she is blissfully unaware of the happy conditions of her existence, Pepe is also lucky to have lived in this cocoon.

There was a story in the newspapers a while back about a woman in County Tipperary who had been keeping five dogs in horrendous conditions without access to water, food or adequate shelter. When rescued, one of the dogs, a Pomeranian, was covered in faeces. It had lost almost all its teeth. It was in such bad condition that an inspector said he was initially unable to distinguish what breed of dog it was.

The picture of the dog would send shivers down the spine of most civilised human beings. It looked as if it had been living in a sewer. The Pomeranian and the other four dogs were taken in by the ISPCA and, in all probability, were put down not long after.

I wonder how that dog owner could have been so cruel. But sometimes I wonder if I am cruel to Pepe. Sometimes I take pleasure in her pathetic antics. I laugh at her as she wanders around the garden lost and disorientated, or when she circles round and round in her bed, perhaps for minutes, trying to lie down in a comfortable, curled position, and then, having found a comfortable position, gets up less than a minute later and starts the procedure all over again. Is she distressed? Not that I can see. She seems to view it as normal. You go round and round in circles looking for the perfect spot and then, just when you think you have found it, you decide it is not as comfortable as you had hoped, so you get up and start the search all over again.

Humans can be equally pathetic. There are TV shows devoted to demonstrating their stupidity. Home videos of a dad falling off a roof when putting up Christmas lights, young men hammering nails into their hands, well-known celebrities eating insects as part of some reality-TV test.

Humans can quickly and easily revert to taking pleasure in the suffering, pain and misfortune of others. It was not so long ago that people went to the local square to watch someone being flayed, burned, hanged, drawn and quartered.

And if there wasn't a human being to kill, there was always a dog. In her *First Friend: A History of Dogs and Humans*, Katharine Rogers describes how, as recently as the nineteenth century in England, villagers enjoyed the pleasure of catching a stray dog and drowning it as slowly as possible. She goes on to refer to Thomas Hardy's 'The Mongrel', in which he describes how a man, wanting to get rid of his dog rather than pay a tax to keep him, brought him to the seaside and kept throwing a stick out into the sea for the dog to fetch. The dog faithfully went to retrieve the stick, but the man knew the tide was changing and the dog, worn out from fetching, would eventually be dragged out to sea and drown.

In the sixteenth century, a favourite form of entertainment, enjoyed by kings and queens, was to watch as a cat was put into a sling and slowly immersed in a fire. They laughed as the cat screamed in pain. Increasingly, such practices began to be seen not just as cruel and unusual, but as barbaric.

Taking pleasure in the pain and suffering of others is one of the things that makes humans different from other animals. Animals may kill and eat each other, but they do so to survive, not for pleasure.

Being Cruel to be Kind

When I was growing up, if I did something wrong, my mother used to say, in an exasperated voice, 'Oh, spare the rod and spoil the child.' Not that she ever hit me, let alone with a rod: but she did keep a cane in the hallstand as a threat that it might be used one day. My father never even raised his voice to me. He disliked any form of violence, incivility or rudeness.

It was very different in school. The religious brothers that ran it used to beat me regularly. I was not alone: everyone got beaten. The brothers had an array of canes and specially made leather belts. Before a beating, some of them were kind enough to mutter: 'This hurts me more than it does you.' Others seemed to take a sadistic pleasure in beating children. I suppose if, as was the case with many of them, you repress sex strongly enough, you seek excitement and pleasure in other ways. We now know that what happened to me and my classmates was mild. In many homes of that era, and particularly in orphanages, industrial and reformatory schools, children were not just beaten severely, regularly and unmercifully, they were sexually abused and raped.

I do not think of myself as being cruel. And yet, I have to confess, I did hit Pepe when she was a puppy. It was usually a quick smack on her bottom after she dug up a prize plant or tore a precious garment of Aileen to shreds, perhaps because she thought it was a rat. I realise now that hitting her was unfair and unnecessary. I have not hit or shouted at her in years. In her old age, I have become increasingly patient with her.

I once clipped my son Arron across the back of the head in a restaurant in Portugal. He was being obstreperous. He remembers the incident vividly. He has forgiven me. It takes time and effort to control the violent streak that lies deep within us. In the past, there was no sense of shame in hitting a child. Now, there is shame in hitting a dog.

One of the reasons regularly given for having a dog is that it helps children to learn to think beyond themselves. It helps them understand about caring and about duties and responsibilities to those who are less fortunate, less well off and more dependent.

I like the idea that dog owners, and animal lovers in general, are more loving, caring, moral and civilised. It is very appealing. But I am not so sure. The Nazis loved their dogs. It is said that Hitler liked to sleep in the same bed as his beloved German Shepherd, Blondi. At the same time, they saw many other human beings not just as inferior but as contaminants that needed to be eradicated.

The Chosen One

I was distraught the day that Darkie was taken away. I lay down on the kitchen floor and cried, every now and then stopping to scream abuse at my mother. Like Aileen, my mother was not really a doggy person and so, quite understandably after this outburst, she was very reluctant for me to get another dog. I had to wait a few years, until I was thirteen, when it was deemed that I would be able to undertake all the duties and responsibilities that come with being a dog owner.

Ferdie was not a designer dog, but he could have been. He was black and white, a mixture of a black-and-white English setter and a boxer. He had a large head which was out of proportion to his body. He looked like a big cuddly teddy bear. He should have had a long tail, but the vet persuaded my father that his tail should be docked. It would seem that the practice of docking tails emerged from the time when it was thought that rabies was spread by worms. In the mad, allegorical way of thinking prevalent at the time, it was believed that by cutting and pulling out the white cord in the tail – which just happened to look like a large worm – the dog would be prevented from becoming infected. On reflection, it was a stupid, heinous act. The practice has gone out of date in Ireland and is now illegal, but it is still common elsewhere and, it seems, often required in certain breeds if they are to be shown.

I left the family home – and Ferdie – when I married Aileen. It was another fourteen years before we had a big enough house and garden to think of having our own dog. Given that I had loved Ferdie, that he was a mixture of boxer and English setter, and that I did not have a fondness for boxers, I decided we should get an English setter. I knew nothing about setters. I did no research. I just liked the look of them. I started to look at the Dogs for Sale column in the newspaper. After a week or two, I saw an ad. The breeder lived in Monaghan. He agreed that he would bring one of the pups down to Dublin for me to have a look.

And so, one night, I drove into Talbot Street in the centre of Dublin and went into a pub. I asked the barman if he knew about a man who had an English setter for sale. He looked at me, a bit puzzled, and then looked around and said, 'I thought this was a pub, but you seem to think it's a kennel.' I laughed politely at his jibe, explained my business and sat and waited. After a while, a man came up to me and asked me if I had come about the English setter. I said yes and we went out the back and into a dim-lit room – and there was the puppy, shivering with fear. He was brown and white, not black and white as I had imagined and desired, but he was delighted to see me and, although I tried to carry out some basic checks, I knew immediately that I was not going to leave without him. Buying a dog is not like buying a fridge or a car.

Frodo was a delightful dog, although, like all setters, a bit eccentric. People used to ask me if I used him to shoot, and then reprimand me when I said I didn't. 'What a waste,' they would say. I began to learn about the breed. He was good at charging ahead of me during our walks, doing long loops to the right and then the left. Apparently he was trying to raise pheasants. But he was easily distracted. He had a fondness for sex. If, on one of his loops, he encountered another dog, he would interrupt his search to have a quick ride.

He was more than bisexual. He would get up on anything. When there wasn't a dog around, he liked to hump the legs of humans. My mother came over to visit one evening and had settled into her chair in the kitchen. I was distracted, cooking. I had given her a gin and tonic and she was happy with the glass in one hand and a cigarette in the other. I had my back turned to her when she called out plaintively, 'Tom, will you call off the dog?' Frodo was humping her leg, while she was struggling to get her cigarette into the ashtray and prevent her glass of gin and tonic from spilling.

I think Frodo died of a broken heart. Aileen and I had gone away with Arron and Olwen to spend Christmas in La Gomera, one of the Canary Islands. Our housekeeper, Mai, who loved Frodo very much, was looking after him. A few days after Christmas, he became ill. Mai took him to the vet, who could find nothing wrong with him other than that his heart was very weak. He told Mai that it was unlikely that he would get better and that it would be best to put him down. When we came home, Mai told us the bad news. I was distraught. Arron was also distraught: his girlfriend had broken off their relationship while he was away. It was his first heartbreak. He was crying. I was crying too, but I was annoyed. How could he be crying about some stupid girl and not about Frodo?

A year or so after Frodo died, we decided to get another dog. Aileen was reluctant, but Olwen, who was then ten years old, was quite adamant. Rather than go and buy on impulse or looks, as I had done with Frodo, we decided to do some research. Aileen wanted a smaller dog, one that was quiet and obedient and did not shed. It had to be a bitch who did not want to hump everything in sight, who would be neutered and, most importantly, would not dig holes in the garden.

Although I was not a terrier type, I was taken by the look of the Wheaten. If we met one when we were out walking, I would ask its owner about the dog. This is always tricky, as owners will always talk up their dogs. It is rare to meet a dog owner who will tell you that the breed is a nightmare and not to get one.

I began the search and soon realised that obtaining a Wheaten was not that easy. We visited a breeder in Cavan in late spring and were told that if we wanted one for next year we would have to put our order in then. The bitch had just produced a litter and the pups were all taken.

Then one day I got a phone call from a man in the midlands who had heard from one of the breeders I had called that I was in the market for a Wheaten. Olwen and I found the place without much difficulty but were dismayed to find that it was a puppy farm. It was made up of a number of concrete pens (previously used for cattle), each containing a different breed. It was all a bit depressing, walking past pens of bitches and their pups, until we came to the one with Wheaten terriers. It was so different from visiting the breeder in Cavan, who had the mother and her pups running around their house. I wanted to walk away, but we had come all this way and I suspected Olwen did not want to go home empty-handed.

The Wheaten mother looked tired and sad. Her hair was dirty and matted. But the pups were beautiful: small and dark brown, as they are when young. The owner said that they were eight weeks old. I didn't know enough about Wheaten pups to know if he was lying. Needless to say, all the pups were cute and came rushing towards us when we entered the pen. I had read up on all the things to do when getting a puppy, but as with humans selecting a mate, there is a connection, an electricity, that brings a dog and its master together. There was one that was a bit smaller than the rest and a bit more timid, and who, as if she knew how to play to win, went straight up to Olwen.

When I checked her over, I noticed that one of the ears did not flop down correctly; it was a tiny bit off. I drew this to the man's attention. He checked and agreed. I said I needed a reduction for the dodgy ear. He wanted to know if I was going to show her. I said yes of course I was. But when he began to do out the paperwork, I told him that it was not necessary. He thanked me and, as a goodwill gesture, reduced the price from €200 to €180.

I don't think Pepe ever minded her dodgy ear. Sometimes on a walk it will get into a flapped-back position with the inner ear exposed. Sometimes it gets to me – an indication of her flawed nature. If it does, I lean down and give the ear a quick flick with my finger. But most of the time I let it go. It reminds me that, like everyone else, I have my flaws.

It has always been difficult to explain to people that, even though her name is Pepe, she is female. (I say 'is female' because I have always had a problem in referring to Pepe as a 'bitch'. In polite, politically correct society, the 'b' word is not permitted. Yet I get the impression that people who breed and show dogs use the terms 'bitch' and 'dog' without difficulty. I suspect that among some dog owners calling a female dog a bitch is a code for being a real doggy person.)

Pepe is not the name that I would have chosen. When we brought her home to Rathgar, we decided that when it came to her name we should have a discussion and then vote. Aileen was quick off the mark: because she was dark brown, she should be called Pepsi Cola. I pointed out that in a couple of months there would be no black hair left, but Aileen stuck to her guns.

I strongly objected to the commercialisation of the new family pet. As a compromise, I suggested we call her Peppy. Then it was up to Olwen, who, wanting to keep up the theme, went for Pepe. She said it was stronger. Arron went a bit sideways and wanted to call her T.A. (the initials of my and Aileen's names). Being divided, we did the democratic thing and drew lots. Olwen won.

The Pet Explosion

I often wonder where my devotion to Pepe came from. Obviously, I am not alone. There are hundreds of millions of dog owners all over the world – perhaps even a billion.

In Ireland, contrary to the norm in the West, there are more dogs than cats. It is estimated that half of Irish homes have a dog, while 30 per cent have cats. The level of pet ownership in Ireland is far higher than in the UK, where 30 per cent of homes have cats and only a quarter have dogs.

The simple question is why I, like millions of people all over the world, spend so much time and effort and expense looking after pets who do not do any real work or produce any income. The answer is complicated, as it is all part of a long-term process of change that began thousands of years ago and which has accelerated in the past couple of hundred years.

Recently, a 14,000-year-old grave was found in what is now a part of modern-day Germany. It contained a six-month-old puppy buried with a forty-year-old man and a twenty-something-year-old woman. In Israel, archaeologists examining a site from a hunter-gatherer society more than 12,000 years old found the remains of a human with his hand around a puppy.

When we look at Dutch genre paintings of the sixteenth and seventeenth centuries, pets, particularly dogs, are included both in domestic and outdoor community scenes. Some belonged to specific owners, some belonged to the street. They were kept mainly for the purpose of hunting, controlling vermin and guarding property, but also as a source of curiosity, pleasure and amusement.

Something else began to happen. Keeping pets in the home, spending time and money looking after them, came

to be seen not just as civilised but as fashionable and honour-
able. Pets became luxury items, symbols of distinction. The
growth of capitalism, which accelerated with the development of a new industrial order in the eighteenth century,
meant that the new bourgeoisie were able to imitate the
manners and lifestyles of the aristocrats, who had been the
first to keep pets.

But as Kathleen Kete shows in *The Beast in the Boudoir*,
her history of petkeeping in nineteenth-century Paris,
keeping pets was about more than just status and class
distinction. It was about a new sensibility, a new way of
relating to animals, of care and devotion. It was about pets
coming to be seen as members of the family, with rights
and privileges.

The increasing number of dogs led to increasing measures
to control them. In France, from the eighteenth century, the
state decided that the number of dogs in the country should
be limited and regulated. Dogs, it was claimed, were respon-
sible not just for spreading diseases but were eating food that
could go to the poor. In 1855, in Paris, it was decided to tax
owners of dogs. There were two classes of taxation. Dogs
that were deemed useful were taxed minimally. Dogs that
were kept solely as pets were deemed to be useless and taxed
heavily as luxury items.

This meant, of course, that only the rich could keep useless pet dogs. Having a pet dog that could be paraded on a
lead became a symbol of wealth, like owning a fur coat, a car-
riage or other luxury items. In some respects, owning a dog

has become the equivalent of owning a work of art, and the more exotic the dog, the greater the admiration and respect. This has been reflected in the development of new breeds of dogs and, more recently, in the emergence of 'designer' cross-breeds. At the same time, caring for a pet adds to the owner's symbolic capital: 'I am worth it, but I am not selfish. I care for dumb animals.' Dog owners, at least among themselves, are respected for their devotion. And in the same way that children who are polite and civilised reflect well on the parents, a well-groomed, obedient, docile and friendly dog reflects well on its owner.

It is sometimes difficult to see social change. It often takes place invisibly but relentlessly, like a tide coming in. In the nineteenth century, horses were everywhere, particularly in towns and cities. In England, urban horses outnumbered rural horses by two to one. It is hard, for example, to imagine a city like New York without cars, buses, trucks, subways and bicycles. And yet less than 150 years ago, there were none of these. Horses were the main form of transport. There were almost 500 horses per square mile. It is estimated that one in four people in New York had a horse.

Keeping a horse was costly but played a vital role in everyday life, not just as a means of transport but, for many, of earning a living. The cost today of keeping a useless pet is probably not much more. Besides the initial outlay, which can be hundreds of euros for a purebred, there is the cost of food, equipment, accessories, toys, clothing, day care, holidays, grooming and health care. This is why they are, mostly, luxury items. The US Bureau of Labor Statistics has estimated that nearly three quarters of US households own a pet, including anything from snakes to guinea pigs, but not counting several million fish. In 2011, the average amount a US household spent on its pet ($500) was more than it spent on alcohol ($456), phone bills ($381) or men's and boys' clothing ($404).

Small Pleasures

Carol and I have our little rituals. I am usually the one who rises first and goes down to make a cup of tea for us both. These days, Pepe takes a while to become aware of my presence. She rises slowly, then stretches and mooches slowly over towards the kitchen. I go down to the patio door and let her out. Increasingly, I have to keep an eye on her. A couple of times recently I have had to run after her when, after doing her business, she veered off in the wrong direction, running towards the lake.

When she has finished her pee and poo, she trundles up the patio steps and follows me upstairs. Carol and I read the morning paper on our computers, and then our books and magazines, until it is time for Carol to go down and make a cup of coffee, which is generally accompanied by a piece of toast with butter and apricot jam.

Once the coffee arrives, Pepe gets up from her bed and comes over and stands beside me. I do not know if it is the smell of the coffee or the jam that rouses her. Maybe it is more about memory and the movement of Carol coming back into the room.

It is in those moments when she stands there, patiently, slightly forlorn, living in the hope that I will give her the last crust, that I realise how much I love her. There is something pathetic about it all, this waiting for a little treat. I know these moments are coming to an end and yet I want them to last for ever. I look into her eyes, but they are losing their depth. It used to be like looking into eternity and finding her soul and being held together in the arbitrariness of time and space. Now it feels more like staring into a black hole. There is nothing. No light. No reaction.

I tear off a titbit and hold it out, and she edges forward, giving a sniff; and then, as gently as ever, she tilts her head to the side as she licks the piece of toast from my fingers. There is the smacking of her lips and she stands still again. I tear off another little piece and then another. I make it last as long as I can. When it is finished, I say the same words I have always said: 'All gone.' She sniffs and licks my fingers just to be sure there is nothing left and then, slowly, she turns and goes back to her bed.

I like it too when, unpredictably, she will sidle up to me while I am at my desk, and I stop typing or reading and drop my hand down to scratch her head: she likes the spot just behind her ears. It is as if, in the middle of her day-dreams, something came to mind and she felt the need to be reassured that I was still here, that we were connected.

The encounter of affection is brief. It lasts only a minute or two and then she shakes herself and heads off. If I am lucky, my fingers will get a little lick of recognition before she goes.

How much does she need my affection? When and why does the need come on? I know that sometimes I feel the need to be held, hugged, touched or kissed. I know that when I am not at one with the world it is good to sidle up to Carol and seek affection. But I don't do it often enough. I have become constrained in seeking and showing affection. I used to be much better at it when I was young. You would think that the older I got, the more I approached death and uncertainty, the more I would need to show and seek the touch of those I love.

A Sense of Excitement

When Pepe and I leave the house, anything is possible. She has no idea what is on the agenda. Each journey is like the beginning of a magical mystery tour.

It could be a trip to a mountain, a woodland or the seaside. There could be other humans, dogs or cats to meet. Recently, most of the time, it has been a walk down Martin's lane. But the world is full of new smells and there is always the possibility of some fresh pee at each halting site.

This is what makes dogs, and indeed cats, similar to children: they bring a sense of excitement to the dull routines of our lives. We are weighed down by protocols, codes of behaviour and rules of etiquette. These rules of behaviour have become so embodied in our being, in our sense of self, that we are embarrassed when we break them. We are free, yet, everywhere, bound by rules about what we should say and do.

Dogs are different. They are able to run about and carry on without any sense of embarrassment. And while we may shout out commands at them, we also laugh and take delight in their freedom. They are what we are not. We don't want to behave like an animal. And yet we long for their freedom, their lack of inhibition.

And this brings me back to the question of domination and control. In my relationship with Pepe, it is I who decides when there will be pleasure and excitement in her life. For most of her life, before her recent decline, if suddenly I got up from my desk and clapped my hands and shouted, 'Walk!' she would bark and jump and run about in circles. For hours every day, she would sit in the study waiting for such moments. I have to admit that I enjoy this. I am her lord and god and I insist on her having no gods before me.

Yes, there have been times when, for no identifiable reason, she has started to bark and jump about and, sometimes, I gave in. But far more often, her efforts to cajole me into an outing were unsuccessful. I might be deep in my thoughts at the desk, and she would put a tennis ball into my lap and, tail quivering, look at me in hope. And if I said nothing, she would eventually give a bark. But unless my thoughts were going nowhere, I would turn down her supplications.

This is what makes my relationship with Pepe different from that with another person: I am attuned to her needs and interests in a way that she is not to mine. I think of her when she is not around. I doubt she thinks of me. She has little or no concern for my pleasure. The uncomfortable truth – and I can handle the truth – is that she is generally oblivious of my cares and needs.

There is also a sense of excitement and intrigue living with an animal. Over the years, Pepe has never bit me, even when I sometimes had to take a big, juicy bone from her because Aileen feared she would not finish it and would bury it in among her plants. Nor did she ever snarl when, at the sound of Aileen coming in the hall door, I had to whoosh her off the couch in the study. Aileen objected to sharing the seat with an animal, even Pepe, and she would have gone mad if I had even thought about allowing Pepe on to our bed. Eventually, Pepe learned to recognise the sound of Aileen's car coming into the driveway and, as soon as the car door closed, she would slowly and nonchalantly jump down off the couch.

Pepe was most likely to snarl when I was trying to get into or out of the car. Maybe it was because it was 'Aileen's' car, and her resistance arose from some kind of territorial battle between her and Aileen. No wonder, perhaps, that she took such delight in sitting up on the front seat and being driven around after Aileen died.

We train dogs not just to make them more biddable but to make them more human, to take the last vestiges of animality out of them.

Pepe was well trained. But I never took my eye off her, particularly with children around. I knew that even the most placid dogs can turn. The animality in her is closer to the surface than it is in most human beings.

What was most frightening was when she turned on other dogs. It was as if years of attempting to be civilised were dashed in a few moments and the wolf that lay deep within her being was revealed. Terriers can be vicious, and there were a few times when I saw her set about attacking another dog. I often wonder what would have happened if I, and the other dog owner, had not intervened. I doubt they would have fought to the death. I think it was more a game of bark and bite until one gained dominance over the other, or until they decided the game of dominance was over and were willing to give up and go their separate ways.

Pepe was particularly bad with Honey, Carol's delightful cocker spaniel. Most of the time, they got on fine, but sometimes, particularly when they were leaving the house and both of them were excited, Pepe would go for Honey. There was a wildness in her eyes. It was some kind of innate competitiveness. She made sure to get a vice-like grip around Honey's throat. Honey would snarl and try to snap, but it was no use. After a minute, Pepe would let go and they would go about their ways, often into the car together. What I always loved about them both was that there never seemed to be any hard feelings. It was as if there was an understanding between them that they were dogs and that dogs will be dogs.

While I am frightened by the savageness that lies within Pepe and other dogs, I am also fascinated by it – and I'm sure I am not alone. This may be part of the appeal of pets, and of zoos and circuses: they allow us to get up close to that which we are not. Wildness is strange and exotic.

New Sensibilities

The Society for the Prevention of Cruelty to Animals was founded in Britain in 1824. It came into existence to abolish dog-fighting and bull-baiting (bulldogs chasing bulls) and also campaigned against the mutilation of dogs (which most commonly entailed amputating their ears and tails). Queen Victoria, already a patron of the Home for Lost and Starving Dogs at Battersea, gave the society her patronage in 1840. She was quite a doggy queen, owning at one stage more than eighty dogs of different breeds, many of which she liked to hand-feed.

This repugnance and disgust towards cruelty to animals was part of a new sensibility. As Kete points out in *The Beast in the Boudoir*, the expanding bourgeoisie wanted to be seen as sensitive and refined and to distinguish themselves from what they saw as the rougher, more uncouth lower orders. People who treated animals with cruelty came to be seen as animals themselves and had to be excluded from good society.

For many English people, this included the Irish. Throughout the nineteenth century, the Irish were regularly depicted in the English bourgeois press not just as unruly and uncouth but as wild and savage and, when drawn, were given ape- or monkey-like features. It was obvious that such animals could not care for animals. As argued in *The Times* (29 February 1864):

> The number of worthless dogs in Ireland is prodigious, one or more of them being bred in every cabin. They annoy passengers and frighten horses by their furious barking on the public roads. Being half-starved since the failure of the potatoes, they go prowling over the country at night in search of food. They attack flocks of sheep and kill many of them. They are a protection to robbers and other bad characters at night, because they bark at the constabulary patrol, and thus give warning to criminals to keep out of the way. Many of them are also kept for poaching purposes, and their owners overrun the country hunting game, especially during the hours of worship on Sunday.

In some respects, there is a link between the recognition and establishment of rights for animals and the struggle for greater recognition of women's rights. Slowly but surely, women began to be seen not as lesser forms of men but as equals. They were no longer traded off in arranged marriages between men as part of wealth and property deals. Men had to woo them. There was an explosion of romantic love in the West in the latter half of the nineteenth century and, during courtship, and often beyond into marriage, men had to be sensitive and respond to the needs and interests of women. They had to learn what women wanted, what they liked and what gave them pleasure.

The more male lineage, property and wealth declined as the important factors in finding a mate, the more couples relied on feelings of attraction, and, in particular, women looked for men who were caring and sensitive. This led to new sensibilities and the need for men to be aware of their power and the ways in which they dominated women.

It is not, then, a coincidence that it was women who were at the forefront of the new social movement of caring for animals. Being devoted to women, children and animals – but not necessarily in that order – became a sign of being moral and civilised and, therefore, socially superior. It may well be that there was a symbiotic relationship between these new sensibilities. Men began to call their girlfriends and wives 'pet'. Being romantic became linked to playing innocent, to being soft and cuddly. We call it 'puppy' love. Being loving and caring became part and parcel of a new emotional sophistication that characterised life among the bourgeoisie living in towns and cities. People became willing and able to celebrate love, to be romantic, sensitive and caring.

We can see, then, how increasing recognition and appreciation of dogs (and cats), and of them having their own particular needs, interests and rights, was part of an increase in awareness of the needs and interests of others, particularly those who form part of our web of meaning, to whom we feel bonded and to whom we belong. The care for animals, particularly pets, was linked to a new awareness and care between couples, between husbands and wives, parents and children.

Kennels

Around the height of the Celtic Tiger boom, Aileen and I bought a house in a village in the south of France. It was a dream come true for her. It was a big old townhouse on a main road. She envisaged family and friends coming to visit and that, sometime in the future, she and I would retire there.

The house needed major renovation: it had not been lived in for thirty years. Aileen leapt into the project, even though she was crippled with cancer. The first summer, the dream came true. The house was full: family and friends coming and going, children running up and down the large stone staircases with their art deco railings. But the dream did not last long. Aileen died the following May.

In the summers that followed, Pepe came in the car to France for the holidays. She struggled in the heat, and so every day there was a trip to the local river to cool down. It was there that I taught her to swim. Terriers are not great water dogs. It is not in their nature. But given that Pepe loved to chase balls and sticks and bring them back to me, I thought that by throwing sticks into the river, I could coax her into swimming out of her depth.

In the beginning, I threw a stick into the shallow water, and she had no problem running in, grabbing it and bringing it back. But when the stick drifted out of her depth, she would just watch it go and then look back at me, puzzled. I got tired of collecting sticks and took to throwing stones. She was quite happy to chase them into the shallow water and became very adept at putting her head under the water to retrieve the stone I had thrown – or some other stone nearby. I was amazed at how long she would keep her head under water in her struggle to pull out the stone she wanted. I don't know how long this game of stones continued, but I remember discovering one day that one of her canine teeth was broken. She did not seem to mind, but for me that game had to stop and so it was back to the sticks.

I began to innovate. I searched for sticks that would not drift away so quickly. I became good at judging the wind and the current, and at throwing a stick so that it would land tantalisingly close to her as she stood at the edge of the area that was out of her depth. She would stand and lean forward to try and grab the stick. And then, one day, the inevitable happened and she went off her feet. She had to turn and paddle like mad to get back to shore. Soon she got used to being out of her depth, and within a week she was swimming out to the far side of the river.

Two summers later, with suffocating heat forecast for the south of France, I decided to leave Pepe behind in Ireland. In those days, Mai, who had looked after Frodo and our children for many years, was quite willing to take care of Pepe while we were away in France.

This went on for some years, but it became complicated when Mai moved into a new flat that did not allow pets. While Mai was willing to take the risk, I decided that it was too much to ask and so, the following summer, I put Pepe into a kennel. The kennel was down in Wexford. It was run by Mary, a friend of Donal, who was so devoted to dogs that at some point in her life she decided the only job she could endure was looking after them.

I explained to Mary that Pepe had never stayed in a kennel before. She was reassuring and told me not to worry. And I didn't worry until I came back four weeks later. I suspected from Mary's eyes and hesitant voice that the stay had not gone well. Mary was so devoted to her task that when a dog was not able to adapt to the kennel, she took it into her house. When it was not able to adapt to the house, she took it into her bedroom. Pepe was in the bedroom.

She was curled up in a ball in her bed in the corner of the room. I thought when I called her name that she would, as usual, leap up and run and jump about me with delight. I edged forward. She was shivering. I knelt down and petted her. She recognised me and licked my hand. I was crying. Eventually, she got up, wandered around the room and went back to her bed. I called her to follow me out of the room.

She wouldn't. I had to go over and put her on the lead. She slunk behind me. When we came to the kennel area, she stopped. She did not want to go there again. I had to lift her up and carry her out to the car. As soon as I put her into the back seat of the car, she became more alert. I went to fetch her bed and pay Mary. By the time I got back to the car, she was standing up and, while there was no effusive greeting, her tail was wagging.

There is a parallel story. When I was about ten or eleven, I persuaded my parents to allow me to go to an Irish college in County Meath. I was very excited until I got there to find a shanty town of Nissen huts. The beds were hammocks. The food was almost inedible. It was like a military camp. We were told the first day, and then every morning, noon and night, that anyone caught speaking English would be punished severely. We were not told what this punishment would be but, in those days, it was common for children to be beaten in Irish schools. We were told that if we were caught a second time, we would be expelled and there would be no refund.

As soon as I got there, I knew I had to get out. After four days, I devised a strategy. I pretended that one of the poles holding up the hammocks had fallen and imbedded itself in my stomach. I rolled around the floor as if I were in agony. The teachers were called. They could find no marks, but they decided to call a doctor. He was equally befuddled but decided that it would be better to be safe than sorry and called an ambulance. I was taken to hospital. Mum and

Dad were telephoned, and they rushed up from Dublin. The doctors told them that they could find nothing wrong with me, that I was perfectly fine to return to the camp. I pleaded with them not to send me back. They took me home.

How Intelligent is She?

I like to pretend that I trained Pepe to retrieve any object I threw for her and to bring it back and drop it beside me. On reflection, I understand that it takes two to tango and, just as much as I was training her, she was training me.

In the back garden in Rathgar, her favourite object was a tennis ball. Often, while reading on the back patio, I would reach down and take up the ball and throw it down the garden. I never did this while Aileen was around, as the ball would often get into a flower bed, and Pepe would trample the flowers in search of it.

Eventually I would insist that the game was over. Pepe would retreat, lie down on the patio or go to her bed. However, if anyone came and sat on the patio with me she would go in search of the ball and then patiently drop it at their feet. They usually got the message and threw it for her, and I would warn them that this could go on for hours.

Often, when we were walking in a park or out in the countryside, if I did not have a ball to throw, she would go in search of a stick. This might take some time. She would disappear off the path and run into the trees or undergrowth, emerging with what she considered to be an ideal stick for me to throw. Her judgement was often not very good. Sometimes the stick would be so light that it could not be thrown. Other times it was so rotten that it disintegrated in her mouth or upon hitting the ground.

Worst of all was when she came across a fallen tree branch in the undergrowth. She would not realise that the branch was perhaps two, three or four times her size. There was no way that she could get it out, and even if she did, I would not have been able to throw it any distance. But, being a terrier, she would not give up. This could take a number of minutes, and sometimes I continued along the path for a distance before realising she was missing. Whistling and calling her was no use: I would have to go back to where she was and shout and scream at her to stop.

There has been some wonderful research done over the years to test the intelligence of dogs. One of the earliest researchers was Sir John Lubbock, a neighbour of Charles Darwin. Like Darwin, Lubbock believed that dogs not only had feelings but also dreamt. He also believed that over time, the more dogs lived closely with humans, the more, as a species, they would develop barks with different meanings.

Sir John trained his dog, Van, to distinguish a blank card from a card with the word 'food' written on it. Every time Van came back with the 'food' card he was rewarded with food. Van seems to have become pretty good at this, but when Sir John tried to extend the range of cards to ones marked 'water', 'tea', 'bone' and 'out', the results were seemingly not so good.

Then there is Rico, the German Border collie whose master trained him to retrieve 120 different toys simply by calling out their names. Rico's exploits were published in *Science*, a leading academic journal, and he quickly became famous in the dog world.

Rico did much to enhance the reputation of Border collies, but research suggests that intelligence is not dependent on the breed of dog. In other words, there is no reason, given proper training and conditions, that an Irish soft-coated wheaten terrier like Pepe could not perform as well as Rico.

Given her retrieval skills with tennis balls, I decided that I would put Pepe through some special training. I set out to train her to fetch the post from where it landed on the floor of the front hall upstairs and bring it to me in the kitchen in the basement. The first part of the training went well. I had no problem in bringing her upstairs, getting her to take up one of the letters and to bring it to me at the end of the hall. I then gradually increased the distance until I was at the bottom of the stairs in the basement. It took some time but eventually, when I brought her to the bottom of the stairs, I would say, 'Fetch' and she would run up and bring down a letter.

I knew the post would come around ten o'clock, so around eleven o'clock, I would bring Pepe out from my study and tell her to go fetch. Her performance was erratic. Was it because she was looking for just one envelope and got confused when there was more than one? Was she looking for a particular kind of envelope, maybe a plain white one, and did not realise that any would do?

Sometimes when I thought I heard some post being delivered and she came down with nothing, I would send her back to the hall door, shouting, 'Fetch, Pepe, fetch!' – only to discover that I had been mistaken, and there was no post. It must have been difficult for her, trying to figure out the mind of her master. I wonder what Rico would have done in her situation.

I finally gave up one day when she failed to come back down to the kitchen. I went up and found her with a rolled-up magazine in her mouth, shaking it violently. I suppose, on reflection, there was some resemblance to a rat.

And so, I had to give up on my dream. When I started the training programme, I had imagined a future day when I would be sitting at the kitchen table in the presence of a visitor, especially someone who was sceptical about having dogs. I would hear the post dropping through the letter box upstairs, turn quietly to Pepe, and say, 'Post, Pepe.' As my guest and I continued to talk, Pepe would go upstairs and bring me down the post and drop it at my feet. Indeed, in an ideal world, I would not even have to give the command, as she would fulfil the service when, with her acute hearing and alertness to new sounds, she heard the post plopping on to the floor upstairs.

Is She Beautiful?

The film *Best in Show* provides a wonderful insight into the world of dog shows – and a good number of reasons why I would never go to one. Or so I thought until, one summer, an opportunity arose to show Pepe.

Aileen and I were on holiday in Kilkee in County Clare with our friends Martin and Susie. Martin, who had established his reputation by photographing rural Ireland in the early 1980s, was always on the lookout for local events that would attract crowds. He is able to wander around in such crowds, quietly and unobtrusively photographing people as they go about their business.

Martin suggested that we travel out to a village where there was a festival. One of the events in the village festival was a dog show. Martin suggested that we should enter our dogs, as the announcement said, 'All dogs welcome.' I am not a great fan of dog shows but thought that this could be a bit of fun.

It was held in a field at the edge of the village. The judges were a local vet and the winner of the Miss Clare competition. They both looked the part. The vet was in a brown tweed suit, shirt and tie. The talented young woman wore a flowing floral dress and high heels and looked as if she was on her way to a ball.

There were about forty dogs and their owners. One local boy brought a collie that looked as if it had not been brushed in years. Obviously, the boy thought it would win on the basis of its personality and talents. He had no lead for the dog and had to make do with a piece of blue plastic rope. It was fairly obvious from the way the dog barked, pulled and tugged on the rope that he was not used to being on a lead.

There were five categories: terrier, toy, working, sporting and whatever else was left. When I looked at the competition, I felt that Pepe had a real chance in the terrier class and perhaps could make 'best in show'. Martin and Susie entered Ruby, claiming she was a Patterdale terrier. Besides not looking much like a Patterdale – she was too small – she did not have much of a personality. She was one of the few dogs that Pepe did not get on with.

In preparation for the competition, I had brushed Pepe that morning. It took a while, as her coat was a bit too long and sticky, as she had been in and out of the sea. Nevertheless, after an hour of assiduous brushing and cutting, I got all the matted bits out. She looked great.

It appeared that the main competition in the terrier class would come from a woman with an immaculate white Westie. The contestants paraded around the field, in the middle of which stood the judges. Pepe was brilliant. She kept beside me all the way, never pulling, and when we were told to halt, she sat beside me obediently. The judges walked around and examined each dog. I was confident of success.

But then something happened that blew Pepe's chance. The judges returned to the middle of the field and the contestants were all asked to make their dogs stand. I did not wait to see what others were doing and so I squatted down on my hunkers and, facing the judges, got Pepe to stand up against me with her paws on my shoulders. When I eventually looked around, I saw that everyone else had their dogs standing still in front of them on all fours.

I can forgive myself. My misunderstanding of the instructions about getting Pepe to stand arose from a basic impulse: humans have always loved when wild animals look and behave like them. We love to see dogs stand and beg on their hind legs.

Despite this blunder, Pepe came second. The eventual 'best in show' was an oversized boxer with whom Miss Clare had fallen in love because, throughout the competition, it had worn a pair of dark sunglasses.

Grooming

Aileen liked the idea of Pepe looking well, particularly when she was out walking with her. However, in the domestic division of labour, it was my job to brush her and, once a month, to drag her into the shower with me, where, despite the flow of warm water over her back, she shivered with fear. A couple of times a year, I would take her to a beauty parlour, where again she shivered with fear and pulled desperately on the lead in order to avoid being beautified.

I sympathised with her. Given that her sense of smell is vastly stronger than mine, it must have been awful to be amidst all the odours of shampoos and sprays. I never allowed them to spray perfume on her at the end of her treatment or, worse still, to put a little pink bow on her collar. It amazes me that people who work so closely with dogs can be so insensitive to their sense of smell. If I had a dog parlour, instead of some artificial, foul-smelling perfume, I would offer a light spray of well-watered pig poo. For dogs to be adorned with a bow and then sprayed with some strong perfume, which lasts for days, must feel as if the grooming torture they had to endure for hours concludes with a tar-and-feathering ceremony.

(I suggest pig poo because I think it might suit her best. But I have to be honest and say that when it comes to poo, Pepe has been always mercurial. Often, when out walking, she would be off the lead and we would pass by all sorts of foul-smelling material that would, at best, be given a squirt of pee. Then, on the basis of an attraction that is beyond my imagination, she would come across some material – it could be poo, stagnant water or the remains of something – which would delight her so much that she would roll around in it.)

When I bring Pepe to the beauty parlour, I talk to the groomer about how I would like her trimmed. The conversation is intense. There is, for example, a debate about having hair fall over the eyes. The ISCWT purists insist on this. However, I have always loved being able to look into her eyes.

At the parlour, there is also a discussion about the depth of the cut, how the tail should be dealt with, the length of hair on the legs and the length of the 'skirt' (the hair that falls down from the ribcage). These details were tweaked over the years and stored on the computer, so that as Pepe got older, I was able to go in and say, 'The regular.'

Getting her hair done was not cheap. It cost at least six times what I pay my barber. Having learned the skills of hairdressing and having honed these on cutting our son Arron's hair and mine, Aileen decided that she could save us a considerable amount of money, and Pepe an amount of distress, if she cut her hair. Astutely, Aileen decided not to consult me about her plans.

And so it came to pass that one night while I was meeting my friend Charles in the local pub for a pint, Aileen set about grooming Pepe. The problem was that she did not have a table at the proper height, or the proper harnessing leads. The result was that she was trying to hold on to Pepe with one hand as she tried to cut her hair with scissors held in the other. It may not have helped that she tried to calm herself during this ordeal by having a glass or two of wine.

When I arrived back from the pub a couple of hours later, instead of the usual smooth two-inch cut, Pepe looked like how Aileen's lawn looks after Pepe had been digging holes in it: a complete mess. Aileen tried to get away with it by describing it as 'a random cut' that produced a wild, rugged look.

Pepe, of course, was oblivious to the stylistic debate and greeted me with great enthusiasm. Maybe she realised that what she had gone through was nothing compared to the ordeal of going to the parlour. However, the reality was that she was a disgrace to the doggy race, and so the following week she had to spend a day at the parlour.

Being Proud

I am fairly sure that having Pepe looking good gives me more pleasure than it does her. I am not fastidious about this. I don't brush her if we are going for a walk in the park. But when expecting visitors, particularly children, I would make a point of grooming her.

I like feeling proud of her. I like it when I am out and about and people stop and lean down to pet her and she nuzzles up to them and they say how beautiful she is and I smile with delight. Sometimes I ruin it all by asking plaintively, 'And what about me?'

When we humans meet strangers, we sniff each other out. We may not smell each other's arses, but we are easily put off by foul body odour. We also spend the first five or six seconds scanning for information about the other, clues that tell us something about the person we have met. First impressions are vital, if not always completely accurate.

It says something about me that I have a beautiful dog who is docile, friendly and obedient. It is the oldest trick in the book. There have been studies that have confirmed this. People who have dogs in a park are much more likely to get to talk with strangers, regardless of whether the strangers have a dog or not.

Many studies have confirmed that a dog is a good invitation to begin a conversation. If a smile opens many doors, so does a beautiful dog. Social life can be difficult, and if you are shy, lonely or depressed, having a dog offers the possibility of an easy, non-threatening, short-term interaction. Another study found that research participants deemed people pictured with animals to be more sociable, happier and less tense than those who were pictured on their own.

This is not to say that Pepe has always brought me honour and respect. In the days I lived in Rathgar, I would walk with her in the park that runs along the River Dodder in Dublin. It is a place of wild beauty among the surrounding posh houses and manicured gardens. There are signs everywhere about keeping dogs on a lead, the need to pick up poo and the threat of a large fine for non-compliance with these rules.

The signs are there for non-doggy people, to reassure them that they have the law on their side. Most doggy people ignore them. The park is a small piece of heaven in which their urban dogs can run free. But there is a form of mutual respect and tolerance. For example, on Saturdays and Sundays, the local soccer team play on a pitch that they mark out in the large central grassy area. There is still plenty of space left around the edges for owners to throw balls and sticks for their dogs. In all my time going there, I never saw a match being disrupted by dogs running on to the pitch. In a well-ordered world, there is a time and place for soccer players and there is a time and place for dogs and, when needs be, each can be in each other's time and place in perfect harmony.

One day, in that park by the River Dodder, I was deep in conversation with a friend. Pepe was roaming freely, out of sight and out of mind. Suddenly, a local politician tapped me on the shoulder and, pointing back to Pepe, challenged me: 'Is that your dog? I hope you are going to pick up whatever he is doing back there.' I apologised to her and, whipping out a plastic bag from my coat pocket, went back and carefully scooped up her poo. As I looked up, I could see the politician glaring at me. I felt like a bold child being eyed by a Mother Superior. Feeling humiliated, I deliberately put the bag of poo into my pocket as I walked back towards her. She stood defiantly in the middle of the path. As I got to her, she asked: 'Are you not going to put him on a lead?' I took the lead out of my pocket and whistled to Pepe. She came and sat beside me while I put on her lead. As the politician turned to walk away I called out after her. 'Oh, by the way, she's a bitch.'

Shaggy-dog Tales

I imagine that, from the beginning, humans liked to tell stories about dogs. Some of the stories we've told about dogs over the centuries are very shaggy. Homer told of how Ulysses, having been away for twenty years, came back home.

When he entered the house, nobody recognised him – except for Argus, his very old and blind dog.

Victor Hugo wrote a poem retelling the story. In his version, the sailor returns home to the dog and whispers his name in his ear and the dog looks up at his master and, for the last time, wags his tail and dies. And then there is the story that Hugo himself once had a poodle named Baron. One night, in a fit of generosity, Hugo gave Baron away to a Russian count. The count took Baron back to Moscow. But Baron was not happy in his new home and so he traipsed all the way back to Paris to be with Hugo.

Another favourite story is the one about a greyhound owned by a knight. The dog was left in a nursery to protect a baby asleep in a cradle. When the knight returned, he found the greyhound dripping blood from his mouth, standing over the cradle. The knight immediately put the dog to the sword, only to discover moments later the baby safely asleep underneath the cradle and, in another part of the room, the body of a large snake that the dog had torn to pieces.

There are endless stories about dogs and their heroic feats and acts of fidelity. They are the stuff of many tabloids. I like the ones where a dog jumps in front of a bus or a train to prevent a baby, or its owner, from being run over. Or the one where a dog took a bullet for its master by jumping in front of a gunman. Or when an owner fell on ice out walking and his dog kept him alive by lying on him and licking him. These stories warm the hearts of dog owners. They reaffirm the position of dogs in society and the love and commitment owners have for their dogs. Most of the images and stories about dogs in the media are about their fidelity, their goodness and the pleasure and joy they bring to humans.

There have been numerous studies that have tried to get to the bottom of dog fidelity and care for members of the family or group to which they belong. It mainly relates to a sense of dependency – dogs need their owners to shelter, feed and care for them – and a sense of pack loyalty. But there is a danger of overstating this fidelity and, worse still, of making out that dogs are almost human in the way they love and care for their owners and members of their pack.

One of the participants in an American study described how, one day, her daughter had gone to her room and the family dog went and sought her out because, the participant claimed, it sensed that there was something wrong. Another day, the participant said she was feeling a bit blue. She was sitting alone on the porch when the dog came and snuggled into her, and she said it was as if the dog were saying, 'If you want to pet me, I'm here if you need me.' There is a saying in sociology that if people believe things to be true, they are true in their consequences. When we persuade ourselves that our dogs love and care for us, then we see them doing so.

Doggy people also tell very ordinary tales about their dogs, much as new parents share stories about the antics of their babies. 'You'll never guess what Bess did today!' helps to create a bond between each other and the baby. In the years after Aileen died, when Olwen was still at school, she would regularly come home and into my study and sit on the couch and we would exchange stories about Pepe. The couch was a filling station for warmth, comfort and consolation. Pepe was the medium for our remaining bonded.

I like to tell stories about Pepe. I like to entertain thoughts of loyalty and fidelity, that if she got lost she would spend days trying to find her way back home, that if an intruder entered the house she would fight to the death to defend me, and that if I died, she would refuse to eat and if brought to my grave would refuse to leave.

I realise, however, there is a danger of humans creating false dogs. There are as many, if not more, stories to be told of dogs savaging babies rather than rescuing them. Maybe the reason why the story of the knight returning home has become such a favourite is because we expect the opposite. I suspect that there are not many parents who would leave a dog and a child alone in the same room. And yet, there was the story about a Rottweiler that killed its owner's infant son. The owner was very upset at the prospect of having to have the dog put to sleep. She pleaded with the judge to change his verdict, saying that while she could always have another baby, she could never replace that particular dog.

Member of the Family

There was an opinion poll published recently which showed that 94 per cent of owners saw their dogs as members of the family. Over half (54 per cent) would consider ending a relationship if they thought their pup did not like the partner they picked. Over half (56 per cent) said that when they came home, they said hello to their dog first, before their loved ones. And just under half (47 per cent) said they found it harder to leave their dog for a week than their human partner. A more scientific study in America, using tested psychological measures, found that people's attachment to pet dogs was weaker than their attachment to their mother, father, siblings or best friend – but only very slightly weaker.

Over seventeen years, Pepe has become a central strand in the webs of meaning in which I have been immersed. She became central to the way Aileen, Arron and Olwen, and later Carol, related to each other. We shared experiences together with Pepe, we told stories to each other about her. We put up photos of her around the house. We shared photos of her through the internet. For my sixtieth birthday, Olwen got a professional photographer to take a portrait of Pepe and me sitting together, staring out into space.

Last summer, while Carol and I were away in France, Olwen took Pepe up to Donegal. There is a photo of Pepe walking on a long, deserted beach about twenty yards behind Olwen and one of her friends. She is walking into the wind, which is blowing her hair back. It is a somewhat forlorn, slightly sad image of an old dog trying to keep up with her master.

The picture does not tell the story of how, when they reached the end of the beach and crossed over into a field, they were suddenly aware of a lot of sheep. When the friend asked Olwen about putting Pepe on the lead, Olwen insisted that Pepe had never chased sheep in her life and that, given her age and infirmity, she was unlikely to start now. She was wrong. She turned her back on the dog and, within seconds, Pepe was running off through the field with Olwen screaming and running after her. Sheep are not the most agile of animals, but they had no problem dodging Pepe. Olwen says it took her ten minutes to catch her.

Many people, particularly dog owners, consider it perfectly civilised to have their dogs eat at the same table – perhaps even from the same fork. I once saw a woman do this in a restaurant in the south of France. She sat opposite her husband at a table for two with a small white dog on her lap. As she chatted amicably with her husband, she nonchalantly fed the dog every third or fourth forkful. Was this a bridge too far? Was she bringing disgrace to the dog lovers of this world? Many people sleep in the same bed as their dog, or even dogs. I bet most of them would be disgusted by the idea of sleeping with a pig. I never let Pepe sleep on my bed. In any event, it was a mutual choice: she never wanted to sleep with me. I am quite happy for Pepe to lick my fingers and toes and face. However, I baulk at the idea of her licking my fork while I am still eating.

Although I am very attached to Pepe, the idea of seeing her as more important than another human being, let alone one of my children, is beyond me. I am dismayed by people who treat their dogs the same as, if not better than, human members of their family or, indeed, other human beings in general. In fact, I think it is unfair to treat dogs like humans. It makes them out to be what they are not. I always think it is sad when some rich person leaves their fortune to their dog. It doesn't make the dog any happier. It is probably a sign of the rich person's own unhappiness.

She Smells

She is becoming deafer and blinder by the day. But she still has a sense of what is happening. I am not sure if it is smell or intuition. Maybe it's a mixture of both. I was doing some yoga exercises in the bedroom and, as usual, she came up and wandered around the bed and found me lying outstretched on the floor, trying to reach my toes. She stopped and lay down at my feet for a while. Then, as if the smell got to her, she edged closer and started to lick my toes. It is where, at times, I get some dried skin. Maybe there is a smell there that she likes. It is a pleasurable sensation as her tongue tries to reach into the crevice between the smaller toes.

It is all very quaint. There I am, trying to grasp my toes, and there she is, licking away at them. Because the stretching movement is slow, it does not disturb her. Increasingly now, when I go to pet her too quickly, she flinches, as she does not see my hand coming towards her. This time, she sees my hand and licks it as if it might be a new set of toes. But the smell must be disappointing, because she immediately stops, looks vaguely towards me, raises herself slowly, turns and leaves the room. There is no need to say a word.

I am still reluctant to put her on a lead when we go out walking. In the same way I might be distracted by seeing a bird or a flower and be taken by its beauty, she can be ambling along and suddenly a smell hits her and she retraces her steps with her nose to the ground. From that moment, she is lost to me. She has been sucked into a sensation and is nuzzling through extraneous material to get to the source. This can take a while. But somewhere there is an essence to be found. It has to be sniffed out. When it is located, there is a moment of stillness as she draws in all of its nuances. It is as if she has found the meaning of her life as a dog. It is the equivalent of catching sight of a beautiful bird or the smile of someone you love. It is momentary and unpredictable and yet it captures the subtle wonder of the world. If she could talk, she would probably talk about the smell in the same way sommeliers talk about the bouquet of a wine: hints of ammonia, petrol, soya and treacle giving a lasting effect that lingers on the nostrils.

Slowly, she unwinds her way back out of the smell and lifts her head. She is dazed, as though waking up from a deep sleep in a strange place. She tries to remember where she is. It is time to go in search of me, but before she goes, she has to add to the beauty and mystery of life and so she circles around the spot one last time before giving it a quick squirt. It is a mystery to me how, when she drinks so little, she always has some pee in reserve for this procedure.

I know I am being reckless to walk her without a lead, because often, when she comes out of a smell, I am fifty yards or more away. As much as she gets lost in her smell, I get lost in my thoughts. As her health has deteriorated, I have tried to develop a routine of continually looking over my shoulder; but thoughts, like smells, can be overwhelming.

She may be seventeen but, when she wants to, she can run like a leveret, bounding along with her ears pinned back, leaping into the air as if she were on a trampoline. Her eyes are shining and it always seems to me that, in those moments, she is smiling and happy. All is good with the world. She has had a great smell and I am there, somewhere in the distance, waiting for her. But blindness is getting the better of her. These days, she does not slow down until she is almost upon me. I fear it will not be long before she runs into me.

Ferdie, the family dog that we had when I was growing up, died from his addiction to smell. Like Pepe, he grew deaf and blind. I never remember taking him for a walk. He had grown up in a cul-de-sac and in a house with a large garden. From a young age, he had learned to take himself on walks around the neighbourhood. I have no idea where he went, but often on the way back he would sit at the junction of Upper and Lower Churchtown roads in south Dublin. He liked to chase cars, particularly slow ones, and in the 1960s and 70s there were still plenty of them around.

He chose his prey carefully. His favourites were Morris Minors, especially when driven by elderly women. They would stop at the junction and, having turned left, would begin to build up speed. Like a lion, he would suddenly pounce into action, bounding along the road, barking furiously at the front left wheel. It was a primal act of great skill and daring. Once he reached the turning for Woodlawn, about 150 yards down the road, he would stop, go over to the wall, raise his leg and have a pee against the lamppost. It was another successful chase to be recorded. He would then amble back to the corner where he started, lie down and patiently wait for the next victim to arrive. It was a good way to kill a summer's afternoon.

Of course, he was hit regularly, and a couple of times very badly, once by a bus. He wasn't chasing it. He was just careless crossing the road. The bus driver was approaching the junction, so he was not going fast. I was on my bike, coming around the corner, and saw it all unfolding. I was sure that he was going to be killed. The front of the bus hit him and he was thrown on to the footpath. The bus stopped, the conductor jumped off the back and we both approached Ferdie, who was not moving. The conductor was full of condolences. But then, as if being touched by a magic wand, Ferdie got up and, ignoring us, began to limp back to the house.

When his time eventually came, many years later, it was a bitch in heat that was his downfall. Aileen and I had a house in Terenure. We had no phone. One morning there was a knock on the door. It was Mrs Batt, our next-door neighbour: my family phoned her when there was an emergency. My mother was on the phone. A neighbour had called to the house to tell her that Ferdie had been hit by a milk truck and was on Upper Churchtown Road. I cycled over to Churchtown, pedalling like mad, fearing the worst. He was sixteen years old. I went up along the road and came across him. Somebody had pulled his body into the kerb. He was motionless. There wasn't a scratch on him, but I knew he was dead. I cried as I put him across my back carrier. He was a big dog and it resembled a scene from a cowboy movie when the bounty hunter rides into town with the dead outlaw stretched over the saddle of a horse. Slowly, I wheeled him down the road, past the bus stop where people were waiting for the bus into town. I could not restrain my tears. I turned at the junction, where he had spent his days chasing the cars down Lower Churchtown Road, into the avenue where we lived, and home.

I buried him in the back garden. My mother said that a neighbour had seen him wandering across the road with drivers swerving, braking and blowing their horns. Later, another neighbour told her that there was a bitch in heat on the other side of Upper Churchtown Road. For days, he'd been wandering blind across the road in search of her.

Am I Talking to the Dog?

When Pepe is ill or frightened, I talk to her. I realise that the words are to comfort me as much as her and that it is the sound that matters. It is a reminder that often, even among us humans, it is not *what* is said so much as *how* it is said. I like to think that I taught Pepe some words during her life, but her vocabulary is rather limited: 'walk', 'biscuit', 'cats'. She is easily confused between 'cats' and 'rats'.

In the beginning was one word and the word was 'walk'. In her heyday, if I used the word 'walk' in conversation with someone, Pepe would appear beside me, her tailing wagging in anticipation. To test her, I would sit in front of her and ask her if she would like to go for a 'W' 'A' 'L' 'K'. but there would be no response. However, if I asked: 'Would you like to go for a talk?' she would leap and jump about with enthusiasm. Sometimes I would ask her: 'Could I talk to you?' She would hold her head to one side as if this would improve her listening. If I repeated it, she would generally assume I meant to say 'walk'. But if I asked: 'Would you like to go for a cat?' there would be no response. After rigorous empirical testing, I came to the conclusion that what made her understand was not so much the word as the pronunciation of the syllables in a particular way, in a particular place and at a particular time.

If I believed in miracles, I would hope that one day Pepe would talk to me. It would be wonderful to know what is going on inside her head. I have visions of her saying, 'All my life I have wanted to be able to say how much I love you.'

I realise that this is all bunkum. Whatever about the brain, Pepe does not have the tongue to talk. It is the same mistake of thinking we could talk to extraterrestrials. In terms of language, Pepe and I come from different planets. Even if she could talk, there would not be any mutual understanding. We have completely different interests and experiences. Just because she has been domesticated, just because she is smart, does not mean that we see, read and interpret the world in the same way. I would have as much chance of understanding her as I would have of understanding an ant, a lion or a shark.

This does not stop me, and most other humans, talking to animals. We are forever putting words into their mouths, making them seem human. I grew up with books, cartoons and films in which animals talked. They had the same interests and concerns as humans, the same feelings and emotions. They too were sad and lonely. They wanted to fall in love and be happy.

Talking to a dog, a dumb animal, should perhaps be seen as a sign of madness, like talking to a wall. Unlike a baby, a dog is never going to learn how to talk. And yet owners do it all the time, in public, without any sense of shame. Indeed, instead of being seen as a sign of madness, it is seen as a sign of being caring, civil and polite. Equally, it is impolite and immoral to shout and scream at them.

Like many other idiots, I still talk to Pepe as if she could understand me. I say endearing things about her, and she looks me in the eye and wags her tail. I try to persuade myself that she understands what I am saying. But I know it is a waste of time. All this talking, all this forcing them to be what they are not, detracts from the main struggle of trying to grasp the way they see and understand the world, of trying to be like them, to think and act like a dog. Maybe I should get on my hands and knees and go down the lane with her and spend a few minutes sniffing at the smells she finds.

Be Reasonable

I have wondered what she thinks about. It is very difficult to know what Pepe is thinking and how she feels.

The main, and sometimes only, thing I have to go on is her tail. When she is alert and exposed to a challenge or danger, her tail is upright and quivering. When she is afraid or despondent, it is between her legs. When she is happy and excited, it is wagging from side to side. As Alexandra Horowitz makes clear in her *Inside a Dog*, there is a whole science to analysing tail-wagging. Not all wags are the same: there is a distinction to be made between happy, tentative and submissive tail-wagging. Horowitz says that when the wagging is more strongly to the right, it means that the dog is familiar with, well disposed towards and interested in the person, dog or even cat it has met. But if the wag is more strongly to the left, it means that the dog is less familiar and less interested in what it has met. I have spent some time trying to discern if Pepe's tail was going more to the right or left but have given up. But I like the idea that if humans were happy, or indeed sad or threatened, in seeing someone, that they could not control their reactions. Maybe they do, and it is just that I am not good at reading their body language. Maybe smiling is a bit like tail-wagging.

We inherit body language. It becomes part of who we are. My granddaughters, Isla and Faye, sit and watch and observe me. They learn so much from just looking, seeing how people are similar but different. How they have different ways of saying and doing, of being. They take it all in, imitating some, adapting others, creating a sense of self.

It is not the same with Pepe. Like the girls, she observes me closely. In the old days, she would spend much of her day following me around from room to room, trying to decipher what I might be up to, looking for any signs of activity that might involve her. Like most other dogs, she got to be very good at this. But it was an uneven relationship. She could never laugh at me and my antics. For her, it was more about survival, about being good at playing the game of domesticated wolf, about reading the actions of her master and the other humans in her life, and then profiting from these skills.

Sometimes I wonder what it would be like to live without speech and rely completely on gestures. I have had some experience of this, in remote corners of the world where nobody speaks English, where there is a reliance on smiles, gestures of willingness and acceptance, deference and submission.

Without language, the world becomes more magical. It seems to me that the world of dogs is quite magical: full of wonderment, full of surprises. Suddenly, out of nowhere, something happens and there is no reason for it. There is not the same sense of, or perhaps need for, mastery and control.

In the early stages of their history, human beings thought magically. They had no idea why things happened the way they did. Sometimes when they were hunting, the animals would appear, sometimes they wouldn't. When they became farmers, sometimes the crops grew, sometimes they didn't. For a long time, humans thought, as many still do, that the world was controlled by spirits. The task was to find ways of manipulating these spirits, to get them to act in their favour. They danced in a certain way so that the rain god would be forced to rain down from the sky. They sowed seeds at certain times, in certain patterns, to force the food god to make things grow.

There is an element of magical thinking when humans say prayers, engage in rituals and petition God's intervention in this world. Sacred objects are used to enhance the chance of being rewarded. People may believe in God, but how, when and why God intervenes in their lives is a mystery. I sometimes think that it must be difficult for Pepe to figure out the random acts of reward she gets from me. She is rational enough to know that if she stands by the biscuit drawer after a walk, she will invariably get a biscuit. But then sometimes, completely unexpectedly, I will give her a biscuit. It could be because I think that random acts of reward make the world more magical and keep her happier. It could be because it enhances my domination of her.

Another difference between Pepe and me is that she has no sense of humour. When I play a trick, perhaps feigning to throw a ball or hiding behind a tree, she is not able to laugh. She makes me laugh, but the laughter is not shared. It may not seem significant, but humour and laughter are important oils that keep the wheels of everyday social life moving smoothly.

This is another difference between Pepe and me. I feel guilty when I have been out and about and she has been alone for hours and I come home late and I am too tired to take her for a walk. I don't think it is fair to have a dog and not to think about and care for it. I don't think it would be fair to keep her alive if she was in pain or not able to enjoy life, just because I lack the courage to put her down.

But I wonder: when she lies alone waiting for me; when she is hungry and would like something to eat and I refuse to give her a biscuit; when she would love to go for a walk and I refuse; does she think that I am being unfair?

Dog Rights

When we lived in Rathgar, Pepe was confined to the basement – a form of social exclusion that was strongly enforced by Aileen. If she ventured upstairs and, very meekly and gingerly, put her head around one of the doors, she'd be welcomed and petted by Olwen or me. She would be allowed to stay for a few minutes to have a sniff around. But if Aileen was there, she would be ushered back downstairs immediately.

Aileen had a gate installed at the bottom of the basement stairs. It was originally to stop children climbing up the stairs, but then it became the gate that kept Pepe from the rooms up above where the rest of the family went to read, watch television, relax and have fun. It was a form of segregation. She may have been a member of the family, but not all family members are equal. She must have seen upstairs as some kind of exclusive club for humans only.

Sometimes the desire to trespass upstairs was overwhelming. If we had people over for dinner, or if we held a party, she often took the opportunity to quietly follow them up from the basement level. I suspect that after a while she began to realise that they, being visitors, would not know anything about the ban and so therefore she could sneak unnoticed into one of the living rooms and get whatever affection she could before being found by Aileen and chased out.

Often I felt sorry for her. She was well behaved and not causing a nuisance. Mostly, people were happy to go on chatting and give her a pat of recognition. But Aileen had this belief that dogs should be in their proper place and that Pepe's place was downstairs. She had created this beautiful house, she was the one who looked after it and she was the one who decided Pepe's rights.

After Aileen died, the ban on visiting upstairs was lifted, the gate was no longer closed. It took Pepe a while to adjust. Slowly but surely, she began to venture upstairs. We might be watching television, and she would come in with her head down and her tail subdued but wagging. But now she would be encouraged to stay, and sometimes she would. However, like many others who have been socially excluded, she seemed to feel that she did not belong. After a few minutes she would slink back out. I liked to think that she was just checking to see if we were all okay.

Now, in my new house, I leave the door to the upstairs and the bedroom open, and even in the dark of night she will come up and find me. She stands beside the bed and I stroke her head and ears. After a few minutes, she will withdraw, shake herself and then move back out of the bedroom, back down the stairs. Given that she is almost blind and that it is pitch black, I can only assume that it is smell and memory of space that guide her back to her bed.

Live and Let Live

Paddy and Anne, Aileen's parents, always got two dogs at the same time so that they would be companions for each other. When I started going out with Aileen, they had a pair of cocker spaniels, Timmy and Julie, and then, when they died, they were replaced by Wicklow collies, Rolf and Zach. They were family pets but, like many other unfortunate dogs around the world, they were never allowed inside the house.

It was not that Aileen did not like Pepe; it was more that she thought she was irrelevant. Aileen had more time for her garden. She would disappear into it for hours. She would get excited about the arrival of new plants and would give a good deal of thought as to where they would fit in. Their contribution to the overall canvas had to be balanced with what was already planted there, its potential to survive in that location, its height and width, its seasonal presentation, and so forth.

Unfortunately, when Pepe was a pup, she thought that putting in new shrubs and plants was a game. In the early days, she used to bury the remains of her half-eaten bones around the garden. So when Aileen dug a hole for a new plant, in Pepe's magical thinking, she must have thought that this was where Aileen was burying a bone. It was a game of hide and seek.

Sometimes I got home early and was able to reinter the plants before Aileen arrived back from work. But there were times when she came home to find her new plants dug up and strewn around the lawn. What made matters worse was that Pepe would run up to her full of joy, wagging her tail with her muzzle filthy with soil.

Things came to a head one day. When I arrived into the back garden, Pepe was on her lead, tied to the railings. When she saw me, she pulled on the lead, wagging her tail and jumping up and down with excitement. Aileen then appeared from behind the large azalea halfway down the garden. I made the mistake of asking why Pepe was tied up. I was invited to come and have a look at the damage. Apparently, she had torn her way through more than a hundred euros worth of plants.

'Something is going to have to be done. I am not having that dog destroying the garden.'

I thought better of saying, 'She's Pepe, not "that dog".'

'She will grow out of it,' I said, without much conviction.

'You should listen to yourself. You have been saying that for more than a year now. Either I give up the garden or you do something with the dog.'

She was right. I had tried bringing Pepe to the holes in the lawn to where the plants had been put, stuffing her muzzle in them and then smacking her behind, while pleading with her to stop. But I knew it was an addiction and that she couldn't. So I decided to press the nuclear button.

I took Pepe up in my arms and said, 'I've had enough of this.'

'What are you doing?'

'I've had enough,' I barked, taking Pepe up in my arms. 'I'm taking her to the vet. I'm having her put down.'

The words came out in exasperation. I was not certain if I was really going to do this, but the rows with Aileen about her precious garden had to stop. It was brinkmanship, a game of Russian roulette.

'You're not serious?' she asked hesitatingly.

'I'm deadly serious. This has to stop. Say goodbye.' There was real venom in my voice.

I was going to say something about waiting for Olwen to come home from school so that she could say goodbye – really throwing down the gauntlet – but there was no need.

'Okay, okay. Let her go,' she said reluctantly.

I knew that I had the upper hand. I decided to take full advantage.

'Okay, I will,' I said defiantly. 'But you have to promise me that there will be no more of this reading the riot act every time she digs up a couple of plants.'

As part of the Back Garden Agreement, I stopped giving Pepe bones, and Aileen halted the planting programme for a year. And Pepe did grow out of it.

On reflection, there was, of course, a strange relationship between Aileen trying to master and control the garden and me trying to master and control Pepe; of her trying to bring the wilderness of an overgrown plot of land filled with stones, weeds and brambles into a beautiful, manicured garden and me trying to bring order and obedience to an animal that is wild at heart and is doing its best to live with humans.

Whistling in the Wind

Her world is getting smaller by the day. There was a time when she would look out from her bed by the window in the living room into the garden and, from there, to the lake beyond, and take an interest in the movements of the birds on the water. Now she has no interest. There is nothing to

94

see. She is becoming blind to the beauty of the world. There is less to get excited about. There is less chance of seeing a marauding cat or fox.

She moves from this bed to the one by the window in the bedroom upstairs. The magic of the world and the endless possibilities it offers have shrunk. I wonder what it must be like to live in such a restricted world, with hardly any sight or sound. I admire her ability to be happy in her own mind and body. Is she happy to just dream? Does she go back to her past and remember happy days? Sometimes I am over-whelmed by the simplicity of her being and go and kneel down beside her and talk to her in the hope that the sound of my voice may bring her some joy and comfort. I hope for a lick of recognition of my concern, maybe a wag of her tail, but more and more all I get is the soft clicking sound that she makes as she opens and closes her mouth.

I am determined to keep her alive, to keep her stimulated. This is why I insist on the daily walk. There was a time, not so long ago, when she was constantly encouraging me to leave whatever I was doing and go with her to walk or play. Now I have to do the encouraging.

The options of where we can go to walk are also shrink-ing. Many of the walks in and around the woods of Lough Key are full of wonder, but they have too many twists and turns. It is too easy for her to get distracted, lose her bearings and run off in the wrong direction. And so, increasingly, I head to Battlebridge and the walk along the canal that runs up to Drumshanbo. It does not have the expansive mature broadleaf trees of Lough Key, but it is open and relatively straight. There is a fear of her falling into the canal, but the path is hardcore and there is enough growth of grasses, reeds and shrubs along the edge of it to form a barrier.

Pepe still takes some pleasure in meeting and greeting the other dogs that strut their stuff along the path, sniffing and peeing, running to and from their owners. I am jealous of them, for they can walk briskly, getting some good exercise. I have to mooch along, constantly looking over my shoulder to see where Pepe is. I get anxious when she is more than twenty yards away. I used to be able to stop and wait and then call her as she came out of the smell. Now I go towards her, gingerly, hoping that she won't come out of her reverie too quickly and run away in the opposite direction. It is a fifty–fifty chance which way she will go, and once the die is cast, no amount of shouting and waving of my arms will get her to stop.

After some research, I sent off for a special whistle. I was disappointed by the piece of green plastic that arrived in the post. Yes, it did make a shrill noise, but I was doubtful it would work. I tried it out down Martin's lane. I got her to sit and walked away, not too far, certainly less than thirty yards. I blew the whistle. There was no response. I blew it again, harder and longer. And again. No reaction. I started walking towards her, whistling away. As I came close to her, she got up and, attracted by some smell, ambled slowly over to the hedgerow, sniffed, squatted and squirted.

It was when I was down by the canal a week later that I finally gave up on the whistle. I had blown it off and on in the house and when we were out walking down the lane in the hope that her hearing loss wasn't the problem, that it was just a matter of getting used to the sound and associating it with me. I was determined that I could teach an old dog new tricks and I was not going to give up easily on her.

We became separated on one of the bends in the canal. When I remembered to turn and look back for her, she was nowhere to be seen. I started to run back, shouting frantically. Then I remembered the whistle. I took it from my coat pocket and blew and blew while I ran. When I rounded the bend, I saw a man on the opposite side of the canal. He had stopped walking and was looking across at me. He looked a little bewildered. I thought about stopping and shouting across to ask if he had seen my dog to indicate that I was not whistling mad. But I didn't. I just took the whistle from my mouth and put it back in my pocket. There was no time for shame or explanations.

The Cuckold

Sometimes I think that I am an idiot, having become so attached to her. It is an unequal relationship. I do most, if not all, of the loving and caring. She is a wolf in child's clothing. She came in from the wild and, as cool as a cucumber, following generations of wolves before her, has insinuated herself into my life. She is a social parasite, expert at preying on my emotions. Over thousands of years, dogs have somehow managed to persuade human beings to look after them, even though, it would seem, we get little or no benefit from doing so.

Imagine if rats, badgers or even crocodiles managed to achieve this. We are constantly told that a dog is for life and not just for Christmas. But what about the turkey? Why do pets have rights over other animals? It must be galling for other animals to see the way humans treat their pets. How did they get away with it? The simple answer is that they became love objects.

My uncle Brian used to refer to his wife as 'the ball and chain'. When he came to visit our family, he would always say, on being offered a further drink, 'No, I have to go, the ball and chain will murder me.' He used to think that he was witty, as many men still do, making disparaging remarks about women. The reality is that Pepe is a bit of a ball and chain, but, unlike my uncle Brian, I am not able to joke about it. I sometimes worry that many people must feel that I am a bit of an idiot when I say that I cannot do something, or go somewhere, because of Pepe. There is a sense of shame of being overly attached to, let alone in love with, a dog.

The truth is that caring for Pepe is not a drain on my love resources. Love is not like money. The time and effort I devote to the care of Pepe do not mean that I care less for others. It might mean that I have less time, but it doesn't mean that I love less. Thinking of her, caring for her, is part of me thinking of others and caring for them. Pepe is not a ball and chain. She is a mirror of my soul.

In 2002, the journalist Kevin Myers wrote a tribute to Traffic, his Wheaten terrier, who had recently died. He described the bonding that had taken place between Traffic and the family cat. Within a couple of years, Traffic had developed a habit of licking the cat's anus. It could go on for an hour or more, while Tensing, the cat, hissed and groaned with pleasure.

Mai, our housekeeper, had a large cat called Tiny. When Pepe went to stay with Mai, she and Tiny got on mainly by ignoring each other – which was hard, given that Mai lives in a small flat. However, everywhere else in the world, cats were Pepe's mortal enemies. She would chase them and sometimes end up in a scrap. She always lost. I often wondered about this ability of Pepe to make a distinction between cats in general and Tiny. But what would have happened if Tiny had come to stay with us?

I am not a cat person. They are far too independent for my liking. Many of them insist on having a cat flap so that they can come and go when they like. I lived with a cat in Amsterdam for two months. I was basically minding the flat, and the cat came with the flat. There was no minding of the cat. My task was to leave out food for him. Sometimes I would not see him for days, but the food would disappear. Then, some evenings, I would be sitting on the couch, reading, listening to music and, out of nowhere, the cat would calmly come in and jump up into my lap and I would stroke him for about ten minutes, and he would purr and then he would get up and go. I imagined him as some kind of playboy, wandering among the locals, getting fed and stroked and dishing out some purrs in return to make the humans feel good.

But there is definite evidence that minding cats and dogs is good for us. There was a big photo of, I think, a Border collie on the front page of the *Guardian* recently. It was a beautiful specimen, well groomed, with soft, warm, wise eyes that looked straight at the camera. It would melt your heart. The photo was linked to a story about a Swedish study of 3.4 million people aged between forty and eighty whose medical and pet ownership records were analysed over a twelve-year period. The study found that people who lived with a dog or dogs, but otherwise alone, were a third less likely to die during the period of the study than those who lived alone without a dog. The report went on to say that owners of dogs originally bred for hunting, such as terriers, retrievers and scent hounds, had the lowest risk of cardiovascular disease. A researcher, commenting on the results, said that if you have a dog, it neutralises the negative health effects of living alone.

The study I read about in the *Guardian* apparently didn't look at health outcomes *for dogs* living in different kinds of households. But the same day, the *Telegraph* reported that a dog that had been abandoned by its owner in an airport in Colombia had died. She had sniffed people at the airport in the hope of finding her owner before giving up the search and lying listlessly in a corner of the terminal. By the time vets were brought in, she was too far gone. She refused food and, despite an intravenous injection, the dog fell further into sadness and depression before dying.

Stuck in Space and Time

Pepe's blindness is getting worse and, with it, her disorientation. She still regularly runs into the wrong side of the door out to the patio. I have to release the door, pull her back and push her out the right side. She scampers off, as if relieved that this small puzzle of life has been resolved. As always, there is no milking of the situation. No anger or any sign of frustration.

It is the same when she blindly runs into things, when she slips and falls. A child quickly learns to cry, to draw attention to its misfortune. Pepe just picks herself up and gets on with it. It is as if she accepts that it is the condition of life to become increasingly deaf and blind, old and frail, to stumble, to fall and to suffer, to feel the pain but make nothing of it.

Sometimes her plight is so pathetic it makes me laugh. This morning, as usual, she came up to the bedroom when I brought up the early-morning cups of tea for Carol and myself. She mooched around the room, perhaps in the hope of finding some morsel of food that had dropped on to the floor. Eventually she returned to her bed and, after the usual rounding ritual to find the most comfortable position, settled down. Seconds later, she was up again, but this time she moved to the left instead of the right. It was a bad move. Her bed is on the left-hand side of the room, between the window and the wall. There is a table in between, and there is a chair in front of the table. The position of her bed, the table and chair has not changed in all the time she has lived here. If she had turned back, then all would have been saved. Alas no, she moved further into the space between her bed and the table. This was bad enough, but then she turned left again. Now she was trapped under the table and the chair was in the way of her getting out. Suddenly, although she was in the bedroom that she knew so well, she was totally lost. It was as if she had disappeared down a rabbit hole and ended up in another world where nothing was familiar.

She stopped and stood still, considering her position. After a long minute or two, she decided to do something. She edged backwards, but she forgot that she had turned and so she hit the back wall. She tried to go forward, but she bumped into the leg of the table. She tried to go left again, but the chair was in her way. She returned to standing still.

I wanted to go and rescue her, to save her from her miserable plight, but I said to myself that she might have done this many times before when I wasn't there and that she would eventually find her way out. Another couple of minutes passed. There was a repeat of the previous actions, with the same result. She returned to standing still. She looked perplexed, forlorn and hopeless. I could not help laughing.

Another couple of minutes passed. From where I lay, I could see three possible solutions. She could back out, but she would have to turn to the left in doing so. She could go forward and squeeze through the space between the chair and the leg of the table, or she could bend down and squeeze out under the chair. As she stood there and I lay in bed looking at her, I wondered what was going through her head. Was she anxious? Did she think that she would never get out of there? Did she think that this was all too much and that it was time to give up? Did she ever wish she was dead?

And then, finally, she found a way out. She crouched down and, tentatively, edged out under the chair. She did it so well that she barely touched the chair. When she emerged, she stopped for a moment, gave herself a little shake and ambled over to me. Once she was reassured that I was still there, she went back to her bed. This time, she quickly found a comfortable position and was soon asleep.

The Stoics were good at accepting the vicissitudes of life, of treating good and bad fortune with the same equanimity. Paddy, Aileen's father, was a bit of a stoic. When he came to stay with Aileen and me in France, he wrote in the visitors' book, 'There are good days and bad days.' When he came to the house the day Aileen died, I asked him if, in all his darkest thoughts, he had ever contemplated Aileen dying before he did. He looked up and, looking me in the eye, said, after a long few moments' silence, 'That's life.'

In the days, weeks and months after Aileen died, when sometimes I would be suddenly overwhelmed with grief, and cry loud and long, Pepe would come and nuzzle into me. I can, and regularly do, make believe that Pepe cares for me, in the same way that I used to believe that God cared for me. I like to think that when I am sad she picks up the emotional disturbance. I like to think that she is reaching out to me, trying to comfort me, and, like a good friend, trying to reassure me that she will always be there for me. But I am not so sure. I suspect that, when I cried with grief, she was able to pick up on the change in my emotional and physical being: she realised that something was up. I am not sure, however, if the nuzzling was an expression of love for me as much as anxiety that the master of all, the provider of food, adventure and excitement, might not be able to perform.

As mentioned, there are many tales of dogs going to the rescue of humans. And there is some scientific evidence to suggest that dogs are aware of human distress, particularly if they are crying, and will take action to intervene. I know that there is plenty of evidence to suggest that after a trauma or tragedy, and more generally with autistic children, dogs can have a calming influence. But is it intentional or is it some unintended consequence?

Honour and Shame

Humans use honour and shame to mould and control behaviour. Children learn from a very young age that if they do and say the right things, they will be praised and rewarded. Their parents bestow kind words, kisses, cuddles and treats, and in school they get stars for their work. On the other hand, if they say and do the wrong things, they will be rebuked and scolded. They may be excluded and made to 'sit on the bold step'. If they show no sense of remorse, they will be made to feel ashamed.

I used the same tactics with Pepe when she was young. When she was obedient, I would sing her praises, telling her she was the best dog in the whole wide world. She may not have understood the words, but she knew from the tone of my voice that I was pleased. I could see it in her wide, smiling eyes and in her wagging tail. I like to think that she developed a sense of honour of being a good dog. That she took pride in doing the right thing.

She also learned over time when she had done something bold. She recognised my harsh tones and raised voice. I would shout, 'Bold dog!' at her and tell her to go to her bed. If she had been very bold, I would pick her up and put her outside the kitchen door. If she had been really bold, I would give her a smack on her bum.

And she did learn, but it was a slow process. Like a child, she continued to do bold things, as if she couldn't help it, as if the animal in her won out. When I came home, or into the kitchen from my study, I would know from her body language, her cowed look, that she had done something wrong. At times, I would have to go in search of the source of guilt. It could be from getting up on a chair and taking food from the table or rooting a book from my bag and savaging it. Sometimes I like to think she developed a sense of guilt. She knew she had done something wrong and there was a feeling of regret. But most of the time I think it was pure stimulus–response. She learned to associate doing bold things with punishment and that it was preferable to be rewarded than to be punished.

I can't know for sure whether Pepe feels something approximating the human idea of 'guilt', but I do know for sure that she does not try to make me feel guilty. She is very straightforward. I can see when she is anxious and distressed. I can see when she is in pain. I know when she is happy. I know when she is excited. I can see when she is shy or cautious and I can distinguish these from fear and anger. These are all feelings that we share. I can imagine how she feels. And, most of the time, I think she loves me, particularly in the sense that she is attached and attuned to me.

One of the keys to being a good, civilised human being is to learn how to control your emotions but also to know when, how and with whom to release them. We learn to let go of pent-up fear, hate, anger and frustration in a controlled way. We shy away from people who scream and shout. But we also shy away from people who hold on to their anger, who deny it and act with passive aggression.

Unlike me and other humans, Pepe is unable to control, hide or manipulate feelings. I can hold back my tears. I can hide my sadness and present a happy face. I can exaggerate my sadness to obtain sympathy. Humans read each other's emotions and play emotional games. It is as much about love and care as it is about power and control.

I should, on reflection, have learned more from Pepe over the years. In the old days, when Aileen came in late from work and her dinner was cold in the oven, I would play the role of the hurt loved one and try to make her feel guilty. I know now that I should have acted like Pepe and greeted her effusively, jumping up and down with excitement that she was back in my life. Making people feel guilty has become a flaw in my character, something about which I am ashamed.

Being Denied

At one stage, Aileen got into power-walking. It was a little bit shameful, as it involved walking around the roads of Rathgar in an exaggerated manner that looked as if she was trying to control her anger – or desperate to get home to pee.

Given that Pepe would not be ashamed of her, I suggested to Aileen that she might take Pepe with her when she went out walking in the morning. This was a bit of a risk. Although I had trained Pepe to walk without a lead, and although she would be well able to keep up with Aileen, the question was whether they would be mindful of each other. Aileen might get focused on keeping up her pace. Pepe might get distracted by a smell and, by the time she came back out of it, Aileen could have disappeared.

They both knew the rules. The main one was that if either of them came to a road crossing, they had to stop and wait for the other. In many ways, Pepe knew the rule better than Aileen. My fear was that Aileen, enveloped in her mind and body, would come to a crossing and power on across the road. My fear then was that Pepe would forget her training and, in her anxiety to catch up, bound into the road, oblivious to the traffic. There were two of them in it. There was nothing I could do, and each morning I lived in dread as I prepared breakfast back at the house.

It was not a surprise when Aileen came back one morning without Pepe. I knew something was wrong because, ordinarily, on the last stretch home, Pepe would run ahead to the house and wait for Aileen to come and open the door. She would then bound into the house and down to the kitchen, knowing that her food would be waiting for her. This day, there was no Pepe.

'Where's Pepe?' I asked anxiously as Aileen came into the kitchen.

'I have no idea,' Aileen said nonchalantly, adding, 'I left the door open for her.' And she turned to go upstairs for a shower.

'What do you mean? Where did you go? Where did you last see her?'

'I don't know. She may be on Brighton Road.' This was the furthest point from the house on the route Aileen took.

I cursed and screamed and jumped about as I dashed out to the hall to get my bike. It was winter, and still dark. The early-morning traffic into the city had backed up on Rathgar Road. I pedalled hard down the road, turned into Garville Avenue, and then straight across the red traffic lights – the traffic was backed up there as well – over to Brighton Square and then up Brighton Road. My mind was racing as fast as I was cycling. Was this the day I would lose her? As I turned the corner, I was afraid I would find her dead or dying at the side of the road.

Rathgar is a city suburb with red-brick houses, tall, mature trees and big front gardens with railings. Brighton Road is one of the posher roads in the area. Many of the front gardens are manicured showcases reflecting the status of the owners. On summer evenings, as we walked round the area, Aileen and I used to play a game that involved stopping and assessing some of the gardens as if we were looking at pieces of art in a gallery. We would give them ratings out of ten. The rating would be based on design and planting, with particular attention to the variety, shape and colour of the plants. But for Aileen there had to be something surprising and challenging to get a high mark.

As I sped up the road, I spied Pepe tied to the railings of one of the houses with a long piece of rope. The garden of this house had been rated an 'eight'. While the planting was excellent – there was fullness and balance between the shrubs and flowers – Aileen did not like the stark red-and-black mosaic of the tiled path and thought the meticulously mowed lawn, with stripes in contrasting shades of green, was too fussy.

As I began to untie Pepe, a woman came out of the house. From her stride and the expression on her face, I could see she was angry. She was spitting fire even before the words came out.

'Is that your dog?' she shouted.

'Yes, thank you. How did you find her?' I asked as I released Pepe, who did not help by jumping up and down with excitement.

'I did not find her. She came in and did her toilet on my lawn,' the woman said defiantly. 'I have just finished cleaning it up. Why don't you keep her on a lead?'

I apologised and muttered something about her getting out the front door that someone had left open by mistake. The apology was not accepted.

'Don't let it happen again,' she said, turning her back on me.

I went home, thinking that Aileen would be full of relief mixed with remorse. She was relieved to see Pepe, but there was no sense of guilt. I made reference to St Peter denying Christ, but she just ignored me.

The next time I went walking with Pepe on Brighton Road, I kept her on a lead. But I needn't have worried about your woman's garden. She had got a spring on the garden gate so that it closed automatically. She had learned her lesson.

I should say that not only do I think that dog walkers should pick up their dog's crap in public spaces, I am even in favour of them being fined if they don't. This is why my coat pockets are always full of plastic bags. Since I've always liked having Pepe off the lead, I have had to be mindful as to when and where she is going to poo. This was where her diet played a crucial role: once her regime of a tin of dog food and some biscuits was maintained, she was as regular as clockwork. A minute or two after leaving the Lakehouse, she does her business. It was the same in Dublin. She had her preferred defecating areas. There was one particular gateway along Lower Churchtown Road that she liked. As we approached, I could tell from the speed at which she was walking, and her gait, when she was just about to make a deposit. Sometimes, if she had been recently groomed, I could see her anus quivering and gradually beginning to open, like a bomber in an old war movie. I became quite professional at timing my scooping. As she squatted, I would reach in and stretch the plastic bag over my right hand and, just as the steam began to rise from the turd, I would bend down and, in one swift movement, scoop it up. Then, with another swift movement, I would pull the bag closed with my left hand, tie it tightly and then gently and gingerly move it into the side pocket of my jacket. This may seem disgusting, but it is less degrading than walking around with it dangling from my hand.

But it was necessary to be vigilant and ready for the unexpected. One morning, Pepe was a little ahead of me and I saw her turning into a gateway. I upped my pace and, when I arrived, there she was with her back arched and quivering while she delivered her load. The owner of the house was just about to get into her car and was staring at Pepe. When

I entered the driveway, the stare was directed towards me. I could see that the owner was about to let fly, but then she saw the plastic bag outstretched over my hand.

'I'm sorry about this, but she is predictable and I never fail to collect,' I said, smiling, stooping and scooping with as much grace as I could muster.

A Mirror of Myself

There is something else about my relationship with Pepe. It has to do with who I am, my identity and sense of self, which, in turn, relates to my sense of well-being.

In my everyday life, in my encounters with others, in my relationships with family, friends, neighbours and colleagues, I feel good about myself by being recognised, appreciated, honoured and respected. My identity, my knowledge and understanding of myself, comes from others.

It is not something I produce and develop on my own. People act as mirrors. I read and understand myself through the way they react to what I do and say. It could be a frown or a puzzled look if they are unsure or unhappy, or a smile if they feel at ease or good about me. Over the years, I have learned that many friends and members of my family understand me in terms of my relationship with Pepe. There is a sense that she and I are an item. Good friends learned, if they invited me to come and stay, to invite Pepe as well. If they were doggy people, I would always be mindful of whether

Pepe and their dog got on. Given that she is part of my identity, I am a little dismayed when family and friends do not ask after her – particularly now that she is old and frail.

I talk Pepe up in the same way that parents do when talking about their children. This is part of getting people to see that she is not just like any other dog. She is special. She has a unique history. There are stories to be told about her, her foibles as well as her achievements. She has her own individual character. I find it insulting, then, when people suggest in a dismissive way that she is 'just a dog'.

It is because dogs are love objects, and because people realise themselves and develop their identities through dogs, that they play an important role in the ways humans interact and communicate with each other. People develop and maintain bonds of belonging and webs of meaning through talking about and caring for their dogs. The dog becomes central to the way they communicate and relate. Once a couple take on a dog, they are no longer a couple. It is a threesome, just as it would be if they had a child.

My realisation of myself as a caring, loving human being is, then, done not just through other humans. It has been through the dogs that I have loved. This bonding, this personal relationship, this ability to realise myself through Pepe and the other dogs with whom I have lived, is part of who I am. It is not exactly 'love me, love my dog', but it is close. There is no shame in loving a dog. For many people, their dog is the most significant being in their lives. They would be lost without it.

Now that Pepe is almost deaf and blind, I have to keep her on the lead more than ever before. This means that I am more directly involved in her pursuit of olfactory stimuli. I have to stand and wait while she settles in on a smell. I have to be patient with her.

But it is difficult. The smelling goes on and on, in and around, up and down, over and over the same spot. To pass the time, I try to predict if this is one of those smells that will be awarded a squirt of pee. Sometimes she just comes out of it and walks away. Some smells deserve a squirt, some don't. I have no idea of the criteria. It is one of the small mysteries of life. As I stand idly by, I wish I could enter her world. I imagine it to be like an enormous swirl of colours and that she is searching out one particular colour that is the essence of all the rest.

And then I get bored with my wonderings and I call out to her and tug the lead, and she digs in with her paws, refusing to give an inch. And then I have to remind myself of the resolution I have made. No more coaxing. No more tugging the lead, even gently. No more squatting down, petting and kissing her head and encouraging her to go on. From now on, she sets the pace. But I talk to her now all the time, hoping that the sound of my voice may provide the encouragement to continue, to get her to enjoy the smell, to squeeze that little bit more pleasure from life.

This morning, the sky looked good when we started out. Yes, there were some dark clouds about, but nothing sinister. And there were plenty of blue patches to make me optimistic. Being early autumn, it was still warm: I had decided to make do with a light jumper. I should have known better. In a magical world of pee and rain, nothing is predictable.

There is no shelter on the lane. The branches of the pine trees at the top of the small incline opposite Kieran's shed are not dense enough to provide protection and, anyway, they are on the wrong side to shield from the westerly winds that bring the rain. It was at the very end of the lane that I got my first smell of rain. I felt the temperature drop. I looked up into the sky and there it was, coming over the hill beyond Joe's farm: a dark grey cloud, almost black, sheets of rain falling from it. Within a couple of minutes, we were both soaked. At least I did not have to drag her home: she ran like the wind alongside me.

As she ran, she may have been imagining her breakfast and the thought of recuperating in her warm bed. But it was not to be. The second we were inside the hall door, I grabbed her and carried her upstairs to the shower. It is a place she hates: the bathroom is the only room in the house into which she never follows me. I suspect that, like the beauty parlour, she sees it as a place of punishment. But there was no time for mollycoddling. I stripped off her collar and dragged her by the scruff of her neck into the shower. There was no reprieve, no matter how much she tried to dig her claws into the surrounding floor tiles. She shivered in fright, in dread of the water about to be pumped over her.

And then the warm water began to calm her. I talked to her all the time, reminding her how good she was, reassuring her that she was all right, that it would all be over soon. And then I came to her face and tried to remove the remnants of the food that had matted the hairs under her muzzle. She refused to stand for it, moving her head up, down and around as I tried to put on the shampoo.

There is a pleasure in washing her. It is redemptive. It makes me feel good to stand naked in the shower with her. Just her and me. It is not erotic. It is not even sensuous. It is more about caring. Standing naked with her – who is always naked – is a form of coming out.

And herein lies the rub. I would find it repulsive to wash the body of another human being, let alone to take them into a shower, to scrub between their toes, clean between their legs, under their arms and then reach into their belly button and take out the detritus that had accumulated within. But with Pepe there is never such a sense of revulsion.

Unconditional Love

I would like to go up and down to Dublin on the train, even for the day. But dogs are not allowed – unless they are guide dogs, or small enough to carry in a bag or a basket. It means that I don't go unless I have to, and I drive. This is not a problem, as Pepe has always been good at travelling in the car. What I mind is the cost, the pollution and not being able to read, write and admire the countryside.

She is a burden, but I can't let her go. I am too attached to her. Sometimes I think it would be great if she would let me off the leash, if she could say to me, 'I'm all done here, Tom. I've had enough. It was good while it lasted. So, come on, let's go to the vet.'

Sometimes I visualise myself doing this, making a snap decision. I imagine myself handing her over to the vet, squatting down and giving her a last pet and cuddle and then walking out a free man. But I can't.

Being in control of her life and death, of being able to decide when and how she might die, gets me down. Her life is in my hands. I am grateful that she is not aware of this, and that, when the time comes, she will go from being to not being without knowing that it is happening.

Why have I become a servant to a dog? How is it that I can have little or no sense of belonging to many of my fellow human beings, many of whom are living and dying in atrocious circumstances, and yet I bend over backwards to take care of Pepe?

I wonder if, instead of giving all this love and affection to a dog, I would be a better person if I gave it to other human beings who are less well off than me. Perhaps my attachment to Pepe is part of a broader social failure: we cannot bond and connect with each other, so we bond and connect with dogs.

There is nothing like death to make you understand and appreciate life.

Many years ago, when our baby son, Luke, died, he had no idea what hit him. He fell from the arms of his babysitter down the stairs and hit his head on the concrete floor outside the kitchen. He was rushed to hospital. There was no blood, just a bruise on the back of his head, which, because he had strong dark hair, was not noticed until it was too late. He had been bleeding internally. His brain was dead.

I have often wondered if he had any awareness of what was going on. Was he in distress? Was he in pain? Does 'brain dead' mean you don't feel a thing? Did he feel anything when they went in the following day to harvest his organs? Do plants and creatures without brains not feel death?

Luke's death was tragic. For a time, it felt like the end of hope. A bomb went off in our lives. The promise of life had been broken. It could no longer be trusted. For Aileen, the blow was long and hard. She did a series of sculptures and drawings – 'House' – that sought to explore how the home, the bastion of love, comfort and security, can be turned upside down and swept aside by death.

Since Luke died, I haven't had a head for stairs. I cringe when I see someone walking down stairs carrying a baby, or standing at the edge of some height. Sometimes I want to go over and tell them to be careful: they might not think that they are in danger, but with one false move, they or the baby they are carrying could be dead. Sometimes I want to scream in my loudest voice: 'You bloody idiot, stop taking life for granted!'

Every time I come home from being out, I open the front door fearing that I will find Pepe at the bottom of the stairs, whimpering in distress with a broken bone or back, or, worse still, dead. I could easily close the door to the upstairs bedroom to prevent all this, but I would be closing off a major part of her life, her sanctuary of peace and quiet. I take the chance.

But, increasingly, she is finding the stairs more challenging. Going down is far worse than going up. Regularly now, I come out of the bedroom, thinking that she went downstairs ages ago, only to find her peering out over the steps, plucking up the courage to descend. She reminds me of those children who get to the edge of the diving board and stand there motionless, as if they have been frozen in time.

The other morning, I heard her going down, and when the trundling noise stopped, I assumed that she had reached the ground floor. But then there were other noises. They seemed to be coming from below and yet they sounded different. I kept on reading, but the sounds continued. After a couple of minutes, I got out of bed and went to investigate. There is a turn on the stairs opposite a window. There is a gap between the stairs and the window frame. It is a small square space about the size of a shopping basket. There is a running board, about a foot high, along the edge of the stairs. Somehow, in her blindness and disorientation, she had clambered over this and was stuck with her front legs in the space and her back legs on the stairs. What if I had not been there to rescue her? What if I had just gone out for a four-hour cycle? Would she have become so distressed that her heart would have failed?

It is the stairs that bind Luke and Pepe together. They are a reminder of the arbitrariness of life. I love life, but I do not take it for granted. It is never fair and cannot be trusted. Life may not be predictable, but we could not live if we thought it was completely unpredictable. I would hate to live in fear, scared by the 'what-if's of this world. And yet, if I am to be stoical, I have to be able to embrace the arbitrariness of it all.

Acceptance

A few weeks before she died, as the sticky buds on the chestnut trees were bursting open, Aileen picked her way around Dodder Park. She was drinking in its beauty, thirsty for nature, desperate to stay alive. She was as slow in her movements as Pepe is now. She was still a beautiful woman, but her bent figure and the walking stick gave her an eerie, frail, elderly look. I can see her smiling through the pain, determined to go on. She got halfway around before col-lapsing on to a park bench. I can still see her looking up at me in delight and pronouncing with a big smile: 'Didn't I do well?'

Most mornings now, Pepe and I are lucky if we get as far as Martin's house. And then there are days like today, when we got to Martin's house and she ambled over to the ditch and began to sniff. And it went on and on. It could have been three minutes or more. I just stood there, like a servant waiting for his lord and master. I have no idea what the smell was, what was going through her nose and mind, but whatever it was, when she came out of it, she set off at a great pace and, to my amazement, we made it to the end of the lane. It was as if the smell was an elixir, a blast that reignited her love of life.

And then, when we turned for home, she started to run. I decided that I had to follow the new rule, that she decides the distance and pace, and so I started to run beside her. As I gasped for breath, I thought it would be ironic if I keeled over with a heart attack.

She is dying. I don't want her to die. I want to prolong her life as much as possible. I devise strategies to convince myself that there is still life in the old dog, that you can teach an old dog new tricks. As the walking declines, her dependency on doing her business in the garden increases. As her control over her bladder and bowel decreases, I have to be vigilant and let her out the patio door regularly, especially first thing in the morning and last thing at night.

It is remarkable how quickly she has adapted to being let out, to inching her way over the edge of the steps that lead from the patio to the garden. There are only four, but for a dog who is almost blind it is a descent into a vortex of darkness. The edges of the patio slates are sharp. She will often turn and look back to me at the door, as if she is pleading for encouragement or help. She looks sad, bedraggled and bewildered, and often I go over and lift her down the steps. But, often too, she makes the leap forward all by herself. She may make it with no bother, though sometimes, increasingly often, she stumbles. I wince. When she is finished, she is like a new dog. Full of life, delighted with herself, she jumps back up the steps, tail high and quivering. As part of this new strategy of teaching her a new trick, I give her a bit of biscuit. It is a small reward. She is no different from the rest of us. As we plough through the tasks of everyday life, we promise ourselves small treats and rewards when we get things done. We train our dogs in the same way we train ourselves.

Last night, I was almost asleep when I heard noises downstairs. It sounded like chairs being moved around. I thought for a second it could be burglars, and then I realised that she must have come down the couple of steps from the living room into the dining room and could not find her way back to bed. She was crashing around the table and chairs, desperately trying to find her way out. I came down and lifted her into her bed. I stayed with her a while, scratching her head and talking to her. When I was finished, I put my fingers down for her to lick: a little ritual we have developed over the years.

If I am downstairs for more than three hours and I have not heard any sound of her up in the bedroom and I think it is time for her to come down for a pee, I go up and gather her in my arms and carry her down to her toilet area below the patio. It used to be that she was distressed if I tried to carry her. She would struggle and try to wriggle out of my arms. But no longer. She is quite happy to be carried, and when I let her down she does her pee, as if anxious to please.

I hope that I may grow old as graciously as her. I hope that I will be as light a burden to people as she is to me. I hope that I am as phlegmatic and stoical as she is when I bump into things or fall down steps. I cannot imagine being as patient if, in the middle of the night, in the middle of my dreaming, I am woken up and cajoled, pulled and pushed into the toilet to pee and poo.

I wonder does she still take enjoyment from life. I can imagine my family gathered round my bed in the nursing home, looking at my decrepit body and wondering the same thing. The only real barometer is her tail. If it quivers with excitement, if it wags with enjoyment, and if she is not in any visible distress, she stays alive. And maybe I will decide that, when she is no longer able to enjoy life, I will invite in the vet to give her the injection while she is nestled in her bed. Maybe this is the way I should go if I too am no longer able to enjoy life, if I become too much of a burden for those I love and who love me. Maybe I should sign up for that now while I am still *compos mentis*.

When she stands beside me and I look down and into her deep black eyes, I have no idea what is going on in her mind. What she is thinking? What she is hoping for? And she steps in closer and I pat her head and rub her under her ear and she wags her tail for a little bit and then she waits and eventually she wanders away to her bed, only for then, minutes later, to come back and we go through the same process again.

God and Dog

I like the idea of God. The concept of an all-knowing, all-powerful entity that is beyond reason and rationality is probably the greatest of all human inventions. It is the basis of most world religions. I grew up in a culture in which most people not only believed in God but believed that He could and did intervene in our lives. This idea of God not only provides an explanation for the meaning of life, it provides hope, comfort and consolation, particularly in times of illness, tragedy and death. I like the idea that when I die everything will be revealed, all the arbitrariness, inconsistencies and mysteries of life, and that I will be enveloped in a love that is way beyond the love that I have experienced in this world. It is a nice idea.

I like to think that, when I die, I might meet up in some shape or form with Aileen, Luke and the many others that I have loved. But even if heaven existed, theologians tell me, dogs can't get in because they don't have souls – so there is no chance that after I die I will meet up with Darkie, Ferdie, Frodo and, assuming she dies first, Pepe.

Maybe the theologians are wrong. If God is love and there is life after death, then it seems unreasonable that there is any limit to this love. The idea of dogs going to heaven could lead to a new religion. Indeed, I have often wondered why in a world in which dogs are loved and adored, there has been no prophet who promises not just a heaven for dogs but a heaven where they will be reunited with their owners.

I am becoming more convinced that it is no coincidence that the spelling 'dog' is the opposite to 'god'. There is a great similarity between the relationship that humans have with God and the relationship dogs have with humans. Throughout history and around the world today, the vast majority of people spend a good deal of time looking for signs of God and trying to interpret what it is that God wants them to do: what is the best way to curry favour with Him; how to get Him to change the conditions of their existence; how to get Him to intervene on their behalf and, most of all, how, when they die, they can get to be with Him in heaven.

This is not dissimilar to the way dogs spend a good deal of time trying to figure out the minds of their masters and how to please them. They are constantly on the lookout for signs of how humans are going to intervene in their lives. While God is invisible to humans, dogs can see their lord and master, but they have the same difficulty adapting their lives to live with him.

Sometimes I run out of dog food and realise it only when we return from the morning walk. Pepe is full of anticipation: she will be rewarded. In my godlike foolishness, I try to explain to her that, in fact, there is no food. What Pepe experiences in these instances is a bit like someone being a good Catholic, following all the teachings of the Church, going to Mass and saying their prayers, and then something tragic happens, a child dies or a loved one becomes ill. And, despite all their firmly held beliefs, they cannot figure it out. Why does God behave like this?

The debate about the existence of gods, of there being one God and the nature of this God, is part of being human. What makes humans different from other animals is that they do not simply live in the world. They search for truth and meaning. And as I ponder the meaning of life, I look into Pepe's eyes and realise that, across the vast chasm of language that separates us, what binds us is the miracle of life. What makes humans different, and has enabled them to flourish, is their ability to create meaning. So while Pepe is part of my web of meaning, I don't think I 'mean' anything to her. There are just feelings of care, trust and loyalty.

As she has got old, I have become prone to giving her titbits. Whatever rhyme and reason there was about treats has gone out the door. The genie of control has been let out of the bottle. Now, any time that I am eating, she comes and sits and waits in anticipation of titbits from the master's table. I like to think that all her life she wondered what it would be like to eat at the lord's table and now she is getting a taste of what it is like. It is as close to heaven as it gets.

I wonder what it will be like if, towards the end of my days, I become like her – feeble, quite deaf and very blind.

Will I take pity on myself and let my dietary regime slip? Will those who care for me give me treats to keep me stimulated?

A Glimpse of Things to Come

Sometimes death comes quickly. But most of the time it creeps up on you, slowly, relentlessly, squeezing the life out of you. We talk about how brave the dead were, how they fought to the end. The great thing about Pepe is that, in contrast with Aileen, she is not in pain and she seems oblivious to the fact that she is dying.

I have had to give up taking her on long walks. Last week, with two friends, we went for a walk in the grounds of the old Rockingham estate, which, after the big house was burned to the ground in the 1960s, was turned into a forest park. The original owners, who developed the demesne in the 1830s, created what would have been the equivalent of their own amusement park. It is full of softcore paths, interspersed with canals over which there are exotic stone bridges. The paths and canals are bordered by enormous trees of all varieties: the English aristocrats did landscape gardening on a grand scale. It is easy to imagine them strolling, boating or being conveyed along the paths in pony and traps.

From the beginning, Pepe was reluctant to get out of the car. In the past, she would jump and bark and leap about with excitement the second the car door was opened. This time, I had to lift her out. She showed some signs of interest but, after a few sniffs and squirts, she began to dig her nails into the ground. No matter how much I tried to cajole her, she refused to move. I eventually gave in and let her off the lead. But she just stood still. I walked away, hoping that she would trundle after me. But not this time. It was as if she was telling me that she was no longer up for these walks.

I told the others to go on. After a few minutes of standing still, I bent down, petted her and asked if we should give it one more go. She seemed to agree and when I started to walk on slowly, she took up her position, walking about ten yards behind me. She has been doing this for some time now. It seems to be the limit at which she still has a sense of me. But what is this refusal to keep closer? Is it a protest? Is it a walk too far? Is she getting any pleasure from the experience, or does she see it as a grim duty? We made it round without too much cajoling or too many stops. It was like being with an incalcitrant, sulky child. I would have carried her, but I knew that would have added to her discomfort. I said to Carol at the end of the outing that it was the last of the long walks.

Two days later, I was walking with her on the lane and, engrossed in my thoughts, turned to find her gone. I ran to the junction with the main road, but no sign. I ran up the road to the house, but no sign. I got to the house and cried out to Carol. She ran to her car. We agreed there was no point in driving towards Carrick and that we should concentrate the search on the road to Cootehall. Carol would drive over to Foxhill and I would get on my bike and cycle up the laneways and driveways to the various houses on the road. We met on the road after ten minutes; nothing. I kept trying to remind myself of all the times when I had thought she was lost and she turned up.

Although we'd seen no sign of her, I felt that she must still be on the lane. Maybe she had fallen into a ditch or got through a gate into a field. I had only just begun going down the lane for the third time when I saw her at the side of Martin's house.

I realised what had happened. She had got lost in a smell and then, as usual, begun to run after me. She had gone past the entrance to Martin's house hundreds of times but, this time, being blind and disoriented, instead of veering left, she went up the driveway to his house.

It reminded me of the time Carol's father, Paddy, was driving home to Dublin from Delgany Golf Club in County Wicklow. It was back in the 1990s and they had just opened a new section on the M50, the motorway ring road around Dublin. Before the M50, there was a straight road from Delgany to Dublin and no chance of confusion, but with the opening of the ring road it was necessary to take an exit to the left. He missed the exit and drove on and on, for half an hour or more, until he came to Dublin Airport, on the north side of the city. While he recognised the airport, he was totally confused as to how he had got there. Luckily he knew how to get from the airport to the street in the city centre where he used to have his office and, from there, he knew the way home.

I have often wondered what it must have been like to be in a world where everything is different but seems right and you have a belief that those who make the roads must know what they are doing. When I asked Paddy what it was like, he said that as he was driving along he felt that he had fallen down a rabbit hole and he just kept hoping that he would land soon.

My Best Friend?

People become attached to all sorts of things: a house, a neighbourhood, a sports team; drink, food or drugs. They can become attached to things that may not exist, such as God. But, outside of other human beings, the greatest attachments are probably to pets.

And this is the problem. I fear that I have become too committed to Pepe. I am not able to let her go. I have created this arbitrary centre of meaning in my life. I cling on to her in the same way that people cling on to all sorts of things — a teddy bear, a pillow, a ring or a mug. If I could, I would let her go. Then I could go and get some young pup full of life. Maybe it is the same with other love objects in my life. Maybe I should have learned from having become so bonded to Aileen. The more you fulfil yourself through the other, the more attached you become to them, the harder it is to let go and, if and when you do, the greater the grief.

They say a dog is man's best friend, and it is reported that President Harry Truman once said that if you want a friend for life, get a dog. But I am not sure that Pepe was ever a good friend, let alone my best friend. The idea of a friend suggests companionship, mutual support, and enjoying shared activities. It suggests an emotional connection – that I am able to see and understand the world from my friend's perspective, as they can from mine; that we can put ourselves in each other's shoes. It suggests that in times of sincere conversations we are able to look into each other's eyes and bare our souls. The problem with Pepe, again, is that it is an unequal or asymmetrical relationship.

Pepe and I are not so much best friends as good companions; we share many activities and we have often gazed into each other's eyes. It is different from looking into the eyes of another human being, particularly a loved one. There is no need for any other gesture, to smile or raise my eyebrows. There is a sense of pure being that I often get from looking into the night sky. A sense of oneness with myself and the world. I have no idea what is going on in her mind. However, the mutually held gaze creates a sense of bonding.

In this respect, it is the same with humans. Our eyes are the windows of our souls. If I am in conversation with someone whom I consider to be a friend and I am talking about something important to me and I believe there is real communication taking place, the spell can be broken if they are easily distracted, if they keep looking away, past me, over my shoulder, or if they look down at their phone or watch. The great thing about Pepe is that she only has eyes for me.

It is this ability of dogs to make eye contact, to hold it and follow our gaze to see what we are looking for, that makes them different from other animals. Research by UK and US scientists, led by the Centre for Comparative and Evolutionary Psychology at the University of Portsmouth, has suggested that over thousands of years of domestication, dogs developed a new forehead muscle that enabled them to perform the cute, doleful look that induces a nurturing response.

Their eyes will get bigger and they may put out their tongues. In the past, it was thought that such expressions indicated excitement or an attempt to get food and, as one of the researchers suggested, 'twist their owners around their paws'. But research showed that the dogs were not engaging in the facial expressions as a means towards an end, but rather to understand and communicate with the human. It showed that dogs' eyes got bigger when gazing at humans even when there was no link to food. It was something that dogs did with humans – not with other dogs. It developed through years of living with humans and recognising the importance of facial expression.

Getting to Know You

I have often wondered, when we were out and about in the park, why it was that Pepe was attracted to some dogs more than others. Some would be dismissed without even a cursory smell of the arse. Until quite recently, the sniffing ritual would sometimes be followed by a game of chasing: the two dogs would charge off into the expanse of the park, escaping from each other and then crashing together, tumbling over on to the ground and then up and off again. Although she tended to do this with younger dogs, it was difficult to predict who, out of all the owners of all the bums she sniffed, would be the one she would start chasing.

I don't want to live like Pepe, judging others mainly by smell, and yet I am jealous of the way that she can run off and play with other dogs with no commitment other than the pure pleasure of the moment, of being alive and happy. In the same way, I was jealous of how Frodo used to be able to go to the park and try to ride any dog that took his fancy. Sometimes I meet a woman to whom I am attracted. I am not sure what the attraction is, but there is a buzz and I wonder what it would be like to run away and romp about.

In the same way that I wonder if I could live with a woman other than Carol, I wonder if I could live with another dog: not a new dog, but someone else's dog. I cannot think of any dog that particularly takes my fancy. In fact, I cannot imagine living with most other dogs I know. I cannot see much of what their owners see in them. But I recognise, and respect, that all dog owners love their mutts in their own particular way. When it comes to love, there is no rhyme or reason.

Dog lovers may find it difficult to love other people's dogs, but most of them fall head over heels in love with puppies.

I like the idea that puppies have evolved over thousands of years to be cute and adorable so that humans will fall in love with them and love and care for them for the rest of their lives. It is no coincidence that we call the first experience of love, which is overwhelming and innocent, 'puppy' love. It is not realistic or pragmatic. It knows nothing about social and economic realities, about commitments, duties and responsibilities. I fell in love with Pepe as a pup and ended up looking after her for seventeen years.

Signs of Life

There was a small brown turd on the carpet beside her bed when I came down this morning. It was the same size as it always is these days. Her strict diet of a can of dog food, and two or three biscuits, means that it is solid and easy to pick up. Luckily, the extra titbits that she is now getting do not interfere with the density. I am getting used to arriving down to poos and pees. It is as if she were a puppy again.

There is some delight to be had from her getting so old and feeble: I can come down in the morning and lie beside her and hold and stroke her head. For the first minute or two there is a clicking sound of her tongue in her mouth and this then gives way to easy, peaceful breathing.

The walk down the road to the lane is slow. When she does not want to go on, she stops and stands still. I bend down, kiss her head and talk to her, telling her that she is a good dog. She moves on, but only for a few yards, and she stops again.

In Paris in the nineteenth century, the new urban bourgeoisie, attempting to make living in the city an aesthetic practice, took to parading through the streets, taking time to appreciate the architecture of the buildings and the displays in shop windows. Some of these *flâneurs*, as they became known, took to walking with pet turtles, the better to ensure they moved slowly. They could have used old dogs.

I have to go to Dublin, and I am running late. Pepe is asleep in her bed upstairs. I could try to wake her and then cajole her into following me downstairs. In the past, all I would have needed to do was shout, 'Walk!' I go upstairs and bend down and pet her. She stirs. I gently lift her up into my arms. There is an initial jerk of her legs. The resistance to being picked up has gone. Now she puts her paws across my arm and sits calmly as I stroke her and whisper in her ear. Maybe this is how she would like to go for a walk. But I would not be able to carry her for that long. Maybe I should get her a pram.

I am sad and weary. What am I doing out here with her? What is this all about? Insisting that she has a walk, persuading her to do something that she does not want to do, making sure that she stays fit and healthy as long as she can – maybe it is unfair, maybe it is cruel?

I could easily phone the vet and ask her to come out some day. I could have the grave dug and, half an hour before the vet's arrival, I could give Pepe one of my sleeping pills. The vet would give her the fatal injection as she lay asleep. Pepe would never know what was happening. Let sleeping dogs die.

Wouldn't it be a nice way to go? To slip away peacefully, in the middle of the day, blissfully unaware of what was happening? I think that Pepe, like most other animals, has a sense of approaching death. But I don't think there is the same dread of going from being into nothingness, from meaning and love into oblivion. I think the only anxiety to Pepe would be having to go into the vet's. That is why I would like her to die at home. To give her a pill and let her slip away quietly.

I am not sure that there is such a thing as a happy death. It may be possible for those who believe that they are going to a better life. But I suspect that even for many firm believers there is some anxiety. Otherwise, they would be blissfully happy to die. We can relieve pain when people are dying. It is harder to relieve anxiety. If there was a pill that would take all the worry away from dying, I would take it.

I am in favour of ending Pepe's life, not because she is in pain, but because I judge that the quality of her life has declined so much, that she suffers so much stress and anxiety because of her deafness and blindness. I am also in favour of ending my own life if I were to be in terrible pain or if I were to feel that there was no purpose or pleasure in staying alive.

The Work of Dogs

There are, officially, seven types of dog. Most of these – gun, working, pastoral, hound and terrier – are linked to the specific work for which they were bred. The other two types – toy and utility – are not bred for sporting or working purposes. Of course, this historical form of categorisation has little or no relevance to most people today. The majority of dogs are not purebreeds and, even among the purebreeds, I would imagine that very few of the officially designated working dogs are ever used for their original purpose.

It would be wrong, however, to say that dogs do not do any work or do not serve any useful purpose. Dogs fulfil vital roles for the owners and the families with whom they live. It is true to say that many owners would be lost without their dogs. The work they do is subtle and often hidden.

First and foremost, they are emotional workers. They are therapists that help people deal with the disappointments, frustrations and anxieties that come from engaging in the outside world. They are emotional sponges that help people overcome loss and loneliness. They help those who are depressed come out of themselves. They are sources of affection and support for those who have been hurt by those that they have loved. One of the best ways of dealing with death, divorce or separation is to get a dog.

The other work that dogs do is to create and maintain meaning. Meaning is built on rituals, and the most important rituals that sustain meaning are the little ones that form the basis of everyday life: having breakfast with family, working with colleagues, meeting friends, engaging with strangers, and so forth.

Like most other dogs, Pepe has become part of my daily routine. The taken-for-granted nature of my everyday life is built around her trips out to the garden, our walk down the lane, her following me around the house, her going up and down to the bedroom. Over the last few months, these rituals have included cleaning up her pee and poo.

Routines and rituals create a sense of bonding and belonging. They create a sense of security: there is a time and place for everything, and everything is in its proper time and place. The home has always been an important backstage to recover from the vagaries and challenges of the outside world. Dogs have become central to the way many humans create and sustain meaning. They help us recover from the slings and arrows of outrageous fortune. Pepe has been a constant source of welcome, company, excitement, play and adventure.

Pepe has also contributed to my identity as a doggy person, part of a broader community of doggy people. We doggy people share a sense of belonging, of seeing and understanding the world in the same way. It creates a sense of collective belonging. We love our dogs and it is okay.

The other contribution that dogs make, as I have argued, is to create a sense of identity and a sense of self. We have become used to marital status as a major form of identity:

people are defined as being single, married or widowed. It might be just as useful to categorise them as non-pet, pet or pet-less. There are many people whom I think of in conjunction with their dog, almost as if they were a couple.

Finally, although it is wrong to think that dogs are members of a family – they do not have the same duties, rights and privileges as human family members – they are a sacred representation of the family. Any attack, mistreatment or slur on the family dog is a dishonour to the family. The collective worshipping of the dog creates an emotional energy that keeps the family together. The dog becomes the emblem that unites the family. Not only do they engage in rituals with the dog, but in worshipping the dog they are worshipping themselves. The dog effectively becomes a totem which unites the family. The dog becomes a little god.

Preparing for D-Day

I phoned the vet today. I wanted to get an idea of what would happen if and when I made the decision to end Pepe's life. I decided to use the term 'to have her put down'. Even though I don't like it, I prefer it to 'having her put to sleep', which is too euphemistic. I thought of saying 'having her executed through lethal injection', but I thought it might be a bridge too far.

I told Maura, the receptionist, that I had been in with Pepe before and that I wanted to know what would happen on the day.

'Well,' she said in a matter-of-fact voice, 'you'd bring her in –'

She was about to continue when I interrupted: 'But she hates going to the vet. It was very distressing for her and me even when she was well, let alone about to die.'

I assume the anxiety in my voice was as obvious to Maura as it was to me.

'Do you provide a call-out service?' I asked.

'Where do you live?'

'I'm on the back road to Cootehall from Carrick.'

'Is that out beyond Hartley?'

'Yes.'

'How far beyond?' she asked.

'About a kilometre,' I lied. It is about four.

'I'm not so sure now, I'll have to ask.' There was a silence and, after a muttering of voices for a couple of minutes, she came back on.

'No, the vet said it would be easier to bring the dog in.'

'Easier for you,' I said, 'but for her or me? You do call-out visits to farmers, so why can't you come out to me?'

'Oh, well, now that would be different.'

'I don't understand how,' I said emphatically. 'Farmers don't bring in cows or sheep.'

It was clear this was not working, and so I changed tack.

'Well, anyway, if I did bring her in, I would have to give her a sleeping pill to make sure she was not aware of what was happening.'

'Do you mean to sedate her?' she asked.

'Yes, so that she is fast asleep.'

'Oh, I don't think that would be a good idea. I'd have to ask the vet.'

'You mean she has to be awake to be put asleep?' I could feel I was going to lose it, so I said that it was not urgent and that I would phone back.

I didn't. I decided I would send an email. But there was no website for the vet, so no email address. It was time to send an old-fashioned letter.

Dear Maura,

We spoke on the phone last week about Pepe, my seventeen-and-a-half-year-old Wheaten terrier. I was enquiring would it be possible, if and when the occasion arose, for a vet to come to my home to put her asleep. I live out on the back road to Cootehall from Carrick, beyond Hartley's bridge.

I realise I am not very different from other owners who have become attached to their pets. My problem is that I am having difficulty calling time with Pepe and I think this relates to myself and my late wife having to make a similar decision with regard to our son Luke thirty years ago.

I would obviously be very grateful if a vet could come to the house. I realise that this is not very convenient and is probably not your policy. I would, of course, be happy to cover whatever extra fees might be involved.

Maura phoned to say that the vet had agreed to come out.

It seems that the word 'pet' comes for the French word *petit*, meaning 'little'. It was used first to describe an indulged child but by the middle of the sixteenth century was also applied to animals that were domesticated or tamed and kept for pleasure or companionship. It was used particularly for lambs brought up by hand.

When my father was six or seven, someone gave him a lamb for Christmas. He had wanted a dog. He said that it all got a bit messy, with 'black currants' being left all over the house. But he grew to love the little lamb. And then, when he came home after his first day back at school, he found the lamb hanging in two halves in the shed.

If it is cruel to end the life of an animal before its time, why are we happy to sacrifice lambs for the dinner table? There was much coverage in the media recently about a man in Northern Ireland who was sentenced to two years in prison for strangling his collie, cutting up the remains, frying them with onions and an Oxo cube and feeding them to his other dog. One witness told the court that she had heard him telling the surviving dog, 'I told you I was going to get another dog and let you taste it.' The judge referred to the 'killing of this innocent, vulnerable dog' and said that 'in any view this behaviour is barbaric'. As he was being led away, one of the onlookers shouted at the defendant, 'Burn in hell, demon! You are the epitome of evil.'

While I would not agree that the man was the epitome of evil – I think that term should be reserved for people like Hitler and Stalin – I think the story reveals how we see and understand dogs. In the same way that we are horrified about stories of the brutal treatment of children, we are now equally horrified about the brutal treatment of dogs. And yet the vast majority of we humans, including myself, are happy to turn a blind eye to the billions of creatures that live short, brutal lives only to be slaughtered to become fodder for us.

Christmas Fear

I'm up in Dublin for Christmas. Even though the holiday is meaningless for Pepe, I have been hoping that she would make it this far, and into the New Year.

It amazes me how quickly she adapts to being back in Carol's house, where Pepe and I lived for a few years after I sold my house in Rathgar. Her routine there is similar to the one at the Lakehouse. She has a night-time bed down in the living room by the fire and, during the day, although there is no specific bed, she likes to go upstairs and lie in the bedroom.

She was sleeping when I went up to check her over and try and comb her as much as possible. It has been a long while since I took her to the groomer. Even though my man in Car-rick is very good – he has her in and out in an hour and does just a basic groom – I decided that I will leave her coat long for the time being. If she makes it through to the summer, I will think of bringing her in to him.

It was when I began to clip the hairs around her arse that I realised that the two large clumps were not bits of turd that had become enmeshed in her hair but two sinister black lumps. I panicked. It was the Friday before Christmas, which was on the Sunday. I phoned the vet and discovered that they would be open that afternoon. They told me to bring her in: there was no need for an appointment and they did not think it would be busy.

I had arranged to have lunch with Arron and Olwen that day. I phoned to tell them of my discovery and that they should be prepared for bad news. As I cycled into town, I wallowed in my worst fears. The vet would say that they are cancerous growths, that they would only get bigger and that, for a dog of her age, there was no point operating.

Olwen did something wonderful shortly after she arrived into the restaurant. She said that she had the afternoon off and that, instead of going shopping as she had planned, she would come with me to the vet. She then began to speak very pragmatically about how old Pepe was and what a great life she had led and that if it was time to let her go, I should do so without regret. In that moment, it felt as if she was something between a mother and a therapist to me.

I cycled back to Carol's full of dread. Olwen, who had taken the tram, was there before me. When I went up to the bedroom, Olwen was lying on the floor beside Pepe, petting her and crying softly.

It was quiet in the vet's and, to my own surprise, I was quite calm. Pepe, on the other hand, was very agitated. She had an idea of what was in store and wanted to go back out the door. There were two cats and a Jack Russell in the queue ahead of us.

Pepe was shivering. There was nothing I could do to stop it. I thought of the time when I was thirteen and I was working for the summer holidays as a delivery boy for a butcher's shop. It was a big shop and they had their own abattoir out the back. Monday was the big slaughtering day. One of my last tasks on a Saturday evening was to go to the greengrocer down the street and gather a big bag of lettuce leaves and left-over bits of cabbage and cauliflower. I would then go down to the abattoir and feed the cattle. Their fear was heart-rending. I would reach in behind the bars and feed them, their big, wet tongues licking my hand. By Monday lunch-time, they would be hanging upside down in two halves.

And then, suddenly, we were called in by the vet. She was young, vivacious and charming. I told her about the lumps. She was feeling Pepe over as I talked and then she crouched down and looked carefully into Pepe's arse. She smiled immediately and said that she was certain that the lumps were just polyps – and they were on the right side of the arse, which meant that they would not cause that much distress when she was pooing. She told me that they could be removed, but she thought the procedure would be too dis-tressing, and I should just keep an eye on them. Olwen and I breathed a sigh of relief. It was an early Christmas present.

The next day, Pepe was full of life. She astounded me. She did the whole walk down to the River Dodder, under the Nine Arches bridge, up to the old Victorian cobblestone bridge and back down along the river and up Milltown hill to the house. With all the stops for sniffing and squirting, it took close to an hour. She seemed to be sending me a message: 'Don't you even think of putting me down. There is still life in this old dog.'

Letting Go

Christmas is over. We are back to the routine of Pepe sleeping and moving between her beds downstairs and upstairs, and me looking out at the lake and wondering what I am doing. The tree and ornaments are down, and I took the ribbon from Pepe's collar. Every Christmas for as long as I can remember, I have wrapped a red ribbon around her collar. It works because she has such fair hair. This year, I had a red lead to go with the collar. Alas, except for that trip along the River Dodder on the day before Christmas Eve, there were few occasions to show her off.

I am full of dark, contradictory thoughts. Once again, I am tempted to send her to her death. There is a pragmatic voice that tells me that she has had a good life, that I owe her nothing. In any event, she will have no idea what is happening; she will slip easily from being to non-being. This voice also tells me, as many others have done, that I should accept that she has become too much of a burden. Death would be in her best interest.

But I wonder how much my sense of my own best interest is behind this voice. There are things, of course, I want to do but cannot because of my commitment to Pepe. I would like to tour around Ireland. I would like to go to Lanzarote to do some cycling. I cannot do either because it would mean leaving her with Carol and/or Olwen. I know that they would be willing and able to look after her, but would it be fair on them? What if Pepe became ill while I was away – as happened with Frodo – and the vet suggested it was time for her to go? Would it be fair to ask them to make a decision that I am unable to make?

Maybe it is not just the burden of care. Maybe it is that whatever pleasure I am getting from her – the odd lick and wag of the tail – does not outweigh the burden of care. I agree with the motto that a dog is for life, but whose life? Does my right to live a good life outweigh her right to life? When there is little or no pleasure and a huge amount of inconvenience, am I the fool for carrying it on?

So I am caught in no man's land: wanting to be free but unable to let her go. The pragmatic voice says that she has had a good life and that I should go easy on myself. But I am racked with guilt. Would I be killing her just because she has become an inconvenience? Maybe I cannot be honest with myself. Maybe I have just grown weary of the pee and the poo, of constantly having to be on the lookout for her, of worrying if she will fall down the stairs when I'm out and die in pain.

And then there is a moral voice. She has some right to life. What right do I have to take it away? I accept that whatever right to life she has is not the same as it is for humans. We kill animals for all sorts of reasons, to eat, because they are a threat, for scientific research and, for some, for sport and pleasure. I think, however, that pets have different rights from other animals. There is a different sense of bonding and belonging, of trust and commitment. They are love objects.

And so, finally, there is the voice of love. I can't let her go. I love her too much. I have become so attached to her. In letting her go, I will be letting go a part of who I am, an important thread in the web of meaning that I have spun over the years and in which I am now suspended. I am reluctant to call it, to do the deed.

I look into her eyes. I am not sure how much light gets in, but there is a softness. The trust she has in me makes me tremble. Little does she know of the dark, contradictory thoughts that I am having.

Poor Paws

I should not have been surprised. I had heard her clacking around downstairs shortly after I turned out the light, though it did not last long and there was no sound of her crashing into chairs. But when I came down this morning, I saw that she had done a large poo opposite the patio door and then, as happened on the staircase a few days ago, she had walked into the poo and tracked it all around the dining-room floor. It took a good few minutes of hard scrubbing to get the poo and stains removed. Meanwhile, she stood idly by, perhaps wondering why I wasn't getting her breakfast ready.

It is a bitterly cold morning. The lawn down to the lake is white with frost, like an enormous Christmas cake. The lake is frozen. It is still dark, but there is a half-moon and the sky is full of stars. Gingerly, Pepe steps out into the winter landscape. You would think that the coldness of the ground on her paws would compel her to pee and poo as quickly as possible. But no, the sensation of the grass crunching beneath her seems to bring her alive. You would imagine that with the cold there is not a scent to be had, and yet there she is, trundling around, nose to the ground, lost in the white world. And, as usual, she comes out of an intense smell and gets distracted and heads in the wrong direction, down to the lake. I have to chase after her, in my dressing gown and slippers, shouting madly, to no avail.

It is becoming difficult to decipher the pattern to her pooing. She used to be regular, first thing in the morning. But in the last week or so, she has been pooing in the afternoon. So when I let her out this morning and she just did a pee, I was not concerned. I decided that either there was no poo within her or else that it would come out later.

But alas I was wrong. An hour or two later, I came out of the study to go to the kitchen to get some coffee and there was a poo at the bottom of the stairs. She had walked through it on her way upstairs to the bedroom. I went and got a bucket of water and a brush and followed her shitty pawmarks up the stairs, scrubbing as I went. She did not like it when I went over to her bed and began to scrub her paws. But, as usual, once she heard my reassuring voice, she stopped struggling. She has always been like that. Trusting, no matter if I was cutting the hair from around her eyes or the lumps of congealed turd from her bum.

My friend Billy called in today. I had not seen him in ages. We talked about dogs and cats. He had his Labrador put down a while back. Billy lives in the countryside. The dog was never allowed into the house. I didn't tell Billy that, according to Keith Thomas, a historian of the relationship between humans and the natural world, this meant that his dog was not a pet. For Thomas, who studied the history of pets in England from the Middle Ages, there are three criteria for an animal to be deemed a pet: (1) it is allowed in the house; (2) it is given a personal name; (3) it is not eaten when it dies.

Billy told me that years ago he had a young Labrador. However, when he moved to Dublin, he was no longer able to keep the dog. He had a friend – let's call him Jim – who lived in Kerry and was big into hunting. Billy thought that this would be the ideal new home for the dog and so made the long journey down to his friend. Shortly after he arrived, Jim suggested they go for a walk with the dog. He had his gun, and one of the tests would be to see if the dog was gun-shy. To test this, Jim said he would simply let off a shot beside the dog. However, the dog did not even make it as far as the gun test. As they were walking along, Jim stopped and pointed to a spot on the ground. Billy could see nothing, but Jim told him that it was a pheasant nest: the dog had walked straight past it. There was no point going on, and so they returned to Jim's house and, while they were chatting away, Jim brought the dog down to a bush, tied the dog to it and then calmly lifted up his gun and shot it.

Being a dog lover, Billy, like myself and anyone who has any sense of respect and affection for dogs, found this horrifying. What was most scary was the quick, matter-of-fact way that it happened. The summary execution was a brutal form of pragmatism. To Jim's mind, the dog could not fulfil the purpose for which it was bred, so it had to go. What is perhaps even more scary is that Jim would see himself as a dog lover.

Another Vetting

This morning, she went out into the garden and spent many minutes wandering about, trying to find her way back to the patio. It was pathetic, seeing her going round in circles, and then, suddenly, as if she had got a sniff of where she should be going, charging off in the wrong direction, only to start going round in circles again. I would have gone and rescued her, but I was in my slippers and, in a cruel way, was enjoying it. I would have felt very different if her tail was not up. It was as if she enjoyed this game of blind man's bluff.

The increasing blindness causes confusion, and often, when I go to pet her, she thinks it is a biscuit and will raise her head and snap. Last night when she did this, I was taken aback and shouted at her. She immediately cowered and went away with her tail between her legs.

I took her to the vet again this morning. There was nothing wrong; I just wanted to get her nails clipped. You would think after all these years I would know something about her needs. But cutting her nails is about my needs. When her nails are clipped, her click-clacking across the floorboards is not so irritating. They used to do it in the beauty parlour, but she has not been there in ages.

Once upon a time, I decided that I would clip her nails myself and I sent away for a nail-clipper. I set about the task gently and cautiously, but she was in such distress after the first two nails that I gave it up.

I was anxious as to how the vet would get on. I need not have worried. As I held her tightly and whispered sweet nothings in her ear, the vet clipped away. It was all done in less than two minutes.

After the vet, I took her for a walk around Carrick. She really enjoyed it, spending up to two minutes on some of the smells. We came to a halt outside the bank, where she settled into a long, languorous sniff. The comings and goings on the narrow pavement meant that people had to step on to the road to pass her. I nodded, smiled and apologised as they passed by. I was not going to drag her away. 'She is always nosing into other dogs' business,' I would say as they looked at me quizzically. If I had had a young pup with me, everyone would be smiling and cooing. Maybe in all this I have become an arrogant doggy man. But who in their right mind would deny an elderly dog a good sniff?

That's the curse of old age. You may get sympathy. You may get respect. People may look after you. But if you become stubborn about the need to take your time sniffing and squirting, they can become exasperated.

In the Dead of Night

My patience is wearing thin. I should be more understanding and forgiving, but it is difficult. Last night we went through the new routine: before going upstairs, I lifted her from her bed, carried her out into the dark, down the patio steps and on to the lawn. She promptly did a pee and scampered back up the steps behind me. I praised her and then threw half a biscuit on to her bed. She spent nearly a minute trying to find it. It was a sad sight. Once she had got it, I turned off the lights and went upstairs, closing the door behind me.

I thought all was good, but I came down to another fine mess in the morning. Shit everywhere. She had walked through it and in and around the living room.

As I went to get the cleaning materials, she tried to get out of her bed. In my frustration, for the first time in ages, I barked so loudly at her that she went to her bed and sank into it with her doleful blind eyes looking up to me.

I apologised immediately. I imagined myself in a nursing home not so long from now, and some crotchety matron bawling me out for having soiled myself.

I felt bad. I let her out to do a pee. As usual, she quickly forgot the scolding I had given her. She was full of excitement. She did her pee and I fed her before going back upstairs with a cup of tea to read the paper in bed. As usual, when she had finished her food, she came on up to the bedroom. It was only later, when I was going back down, that I discovered more shit on the stairs.

The difference between cleaning up after her now and when she was a puppy is that back then there was hope. She would learn. There would be an end to the messiness. And she did learn, quite quickly. But there is no possibility of learning now. There is just the horrible business of shit everywhere.

The next night, it snowed. In the morning, everything was white. I let her out. At first, she just stood there, confused, sniffing the air. I lifted her down the steps. And then her tail lifted and I could sense the excitement, and she threaded her way out into the white wilderness and, wonders of wonders, within minutes she did a pee and a poo. I sighed with relief. And then I saw her disappear off down the garden. The snow must have added to her disorientation. I grabbed my wellingtons and charged off after her. I grabbed her and pulled her after me, but she broke free and headed towards the lake. I ran after her, my brown dressing gown flapping about me. I grabbed her again and this time carried her back. I laughed at myself and whispered in her ear that we are both pathetic creatures.

It is hard to know if she is in distress. Sometimes when I am sitting down at the window in the dining area that overlooks the lake, she gets addled. She is not used to me being there. So she goes up to her bed, wanders around the couch and then comes down the steps to the lower level. She comes over, sees where I am and then begins her wandering again. The click-clacking of her nails on the floorboards is increasingly irritating. It disturbs the peace. I try to continue reading, but the clacking gets to me: I wish she could just settle down. And then I realise it is my own fault. I rarely sit down in this part of the room. She is anxious and confused.

Her habit of going round and round in circles before settling into a comfortable position in her bed has become extreme in the last week or two. I cannot bear to watch her engaging in this rounding ritual. She seems to get comfortable but then is up at it again within minutes. I want to help her. I have started lifting her and placing her in her bed in a way that her whole body and head are in the bed. I then comfort her by petting and talking to her. In the past, she would have got up, uncertain of what I was trying to do. Now, if I keep her there long enough, she stays put, as if she accepts that I am acting in her best interests and she is wrong to struggle and not trust me. Maybe it is good practice for when the final needle goes in.

I had a nightmare last night. It was of a young dog, my dog but not Pepe, not much more than a year old, going crazy in a park, attacking and biting people. It was on a lead, but I could not restrain it. Then it turned on me and, after a struggle, I managed to subdue it, using all my might to hold it down. I shouted at a man to get me a rock, and when he came back with one, I got him to hold the dog down while I bashed in its head. After a few blows, its head was a mess but, then, suddenly, it began to whimper. It was then that I woke up.

I don't dream of Pepe very much, and that was certainly the first nightmare, other than ones of losing her. I wonder if I will dream of her after she dies. I wonder if I will have the same sort of horrendous nightmares that I had after Aileen died.

Fear of Dying

I hate the idea that it is I who will decide whether she lives or dies, the sense of playing God. And yet I would hate to sit around and watch her die, distressed and suffering. And then I say to myself that she is just an animal. In the natural world, many old animals would die a horrible death, being torn limb from limb.

I do not want her to be fearful when she is dying. I do not want her to be in pain.

I'd rather not be in pain myself, when my time comes. I have this dream that death could be pleasant and comforting, like slipping into a warm bath. Imagine if I had a lord and master who decided that it was time for me to go and slipped me a Mickey Finn before I went to bed. At the moment, Carol is my lord and master. She often tells me that I am falling asleep at the television and that I should go to bed. But imagine if she, or some of my other loved ones, decided it was not just time to go to bed but to go to sleep for ever?

It is not so much death of which I am afraid as not being able to choose the circumstances of my dying. Wouldn't it be great if I began to think that I have had enough and that it was time for me to go and that I could decide on a death day? I could send out invitations to family, friends and loved ones. It would be different from a funeral because I would be able to slip away watching all those I love and care for laughing and being happy. It might be a far better experience than listening to them weeping as they intoned endless decades of the Rosary.

I aspire to being stoical about death, to seeing life and death as opposite sides of the same coin. I am attracted to the idea that, in order to live a good life, it is necessary to develop a realistic awareness of inevitable death, to always be accepting and prepared for it. The ability to die a good death is related to the ability to live life to the full, to flourish in the experience of life, to be more accepting of its arbitrariness. Maybe dogs live a good life because they don't dwell on the past or fret about the future and are more open to living in the moment. It may well be that Pepe has become the prism through which I see and understand my own death. I hope I will be able, like her, to see life as a source of awe and excitement even when I am frail and my senses start deserting me. The task is to be anchored and attached to loved ones (including dogs), to take pleasure in small things, and to be willing and able to pull up the anchor when it is time to go.

I remember reading an article about a man who lived in the south-east of England. He had decided that on this particular Saturday morning he was going to bring his dog, Walnut, to the vet to have him put down. He had told his friends and neighbours that he was going to take him for a last walk on the local beach. And so, that morning, they gathered on the beach to say goodbye to Walnut. Word of this gathering reached the local newspaper, which sent a photographer and reporter, and the story and picture ended up in national and international papers.

There was nothing beautiful about the dog, the owner or the beach. It could have been any dog, anywhere. But what made it poignant – what made it news – was the idea that this was his death day. Although the dog had no idea that it was his last day, all the humans did. It was a form of bonding for them, of like-minded doggy people coming together to celebrate Walnut's life and to help his owner cope with the loss.

For humans, death is one of the biggest challenges to the frail webs of meaning that we spin in our lives. We know what life is like, but we have no idea what happens when we die. We wonder what it is like to step into the abyss, to leave behind all the webs of meaning in which we are suspended, which we have helped to create.

Pepe's approach to old age is a source of intrigue and inspiration. She is so noble in the way she accepts the conditions of her existence, her frailty, her deafness and blindness. There seems to be no fear of the future, or of dying. This means I don't have to worry, as I would with an old and ailing human, about adding to her anxiety, about not saying or doing the right thing. I don't have to tiptoe around the issue of her death.

Preparing for Death

So, I have eventually made the decision. It is time for her to go.

It is a combination of things: she can no longer scratch herself; she regularly stumbles and falls over when she is straining to do a poo; she finds it increasingly difficult to get comfortable in her bed. She does not seem to be in any pain. Her mood has not changed. She does not yelp. She does not get angry. She seems to accept the conditions of her existence. But is it worth it to continue living when there is little, other than food, that interests her, that makes her tail wag? Over the past couple of weeks, I have talked earnestly with Carol, Olwen, Arron and his wife, Jenni, Carol's daughter, Greer, and Greer's partner, Simon, about the decision. It was really about me hearing my own rationale and obtaining their reassurance that I have made the right decision.

The next question is what would be the best death day. I have been rethinking the idea of the vet coming out to the house. I had envisaged the vet calling out on a Saturday morning. It would mean that Carol and perhaps even Olwen could be here with me. In that scenario, I would give Pepe a sleeping pill an hour in advance. She would be asleep in her bed by the window when the vet called. We would chat a little. The vet would say nice things about Pepe, I would be a little tearful and then the vet would put on her white gloves and reach into her bag for the instrument of death. I would pet Pepe, just in case the needle caused her to wake up. Then, the vet would withdraw and I would kneel beside Pepe until her life had drained away.

But I began to see a flaw in all of this. People around here have a very flexible approach to time and appointments: it is part of a rural life–work balance. The vet could be an hour late, maybe two, maybe even more. What if Pepe awoke? Would I have to give her another sleeping pill? There was another problem. In the depths of my urban self-centredness, I had forgotten it was spring. Any vet who was on call on a Saturday was likely to be busy with cows calving, ewes lambing and mares foaling.

As well as being worried about the vet not being able to come when I wanted, I was also having second thoughts about being with Pepe when she died: I wasn't sure I'd be able to get through it. So I devised a new death plan. I would go to the vet the previous day, talk the plan through, pay for the procedure and the cremation and get the sleeping pill.

I'd be able to spend time with Pepe on her death day and plan her last meal. I would give her the pill at home, and then put her in the back of the car and drive to Carrick. I would park in the yard behind the vet's a bit before six in the evening, closing time, when it would be perhaps less busy. I would leave the sleeping Pepe in the unlocked car and go for a coffee in the café across the road. The vet would come out to the car and give Pepe the injection. When Pepe was dead, the vet would take her from the car. She would then text me to tell me that the deed was done.

I phoned the vet's office, and Maura said that all of what I had planned sounded good but she would have to run it past the vet. I texted Olwen: 'So decision time and it looks like Friday for Pepe and even as I type this, tears well up. Love Dad'. I waited over an hour for her reply: 'Not a very nice message to get in the middle of a meeting! What time on Friday?' I had forgotten how much a blow this would be for Olwen. She was hurt. Later, we talked on the phone and she said she would take the day off work and come down to be with me.

Death Day

It is raining heavily. The weather matches my mood: there will be tears. Needless to say, Pepe has no idea what is going on. She was in great form when I came down, full of the joys of spring. There was not a stain on the floor. It seemed that her tail was quivering more than usual with excitement. She went out into the rain, scampering down the steps without a bother, and did her business quickly. If I didn't know better, I might think she was trying to tell me there was no need to rush into this death thing.

She came and stood beside me and the tears welled up. She let me pet her, just for a few seconds, and then she wandered off. She ate her last breakfast with great enthusiasm. Then, once she was satisfied that I was installed in my study, she wandered up to the bedroom. Just another day in the life of an old dog.

I don't want to do anything different today. I don't want her to suspect anything. I certainly don't want to cry in front of her. The pills the vet gave me sit on my desk beside the computer.

I realise that many people would think that this sentimentality about a dog is too much: a self-indulgence for the mollycoddled middle classes living in prosperous parts of the world. Those living in dire poverty or in war zones may not have the time or space to prepare for the loss of a dog in the way that I have been preparing, or to grieve in the way that I am grieving.

I reflect on my own life. I have lived in a cocoon of love and happiness. While I have endured illness and tragedy, I have always been surrounded by loved ones who have helped me recover. I think it is this ability to love and care that makes human beings unique.

But the failure of the human project, the failure of reason, is that we cannot love everyone. We cannot live in peace and harmony. Love seems to breed fear and hate. We cannot love our own without fearing and hating others.

We are divided into families, clans, tribes, religions and nations. We can love strangers and those who are different, but most of us do our loving with members of our own group. We fall into the trap of fearing others. We see them as a threat. They are not just different but inferior. 'We' are morally superior to 'them'.

The problem, of course, is that we humans see ourselves as superior not just to others but to all other species. I have never had any doubt that I am superior to Pepe. I may have loved her, but I have also dominated her. I may have engaged in what Olwen describes as 'palliative care', but it has been on my terms.

And yet it is not an instrumental relationship. If I had been operating on the theory of diminishing marginal tail-wags, I would have had her put down ages ago. I would have left her for some young pup. Instead, like most pet owners, I have been operating on the belief that she was entitled to be cared for in her old age.

The Final Moments

At five o'clock, I put the two pills into a piece of butter, which she gobbled down. I had cut up the remainder of some roast sirloin of beef into small pieces and put them one by one into the palm of my hand and let her lick them from it.

If she were intelligent, she would have smelled a rat, being fed such lovely meat in the middle of the afternoon. If ever some loved one starts to feed me glasses of Châteauneuf-du-Pape in the middle of the day, without warning, without anything to celebrate, simply on the basis that I deserve it, I will think twice before swallowing them.

I can still feel her tongue on my hand as she gently licked the pieces of meat from it. I can still see the look of disappointment on her face when it was finished. I can still hear the words that I always said after giving her a treat: 'All gone.' And I can still see her smacking her lips and looking down and then sniffing the floor to make sure some small morsel had not slipped from her mouth.

Olwen and I then waited for the pills to take effect. I had imagined that she would fall asleep in her bed by the window overlooking the lake and we would then carry her out and put her on the back seat of the car. Alas, the pills made her listless but did not put her to sleep, and she did her usual routine of walking round and round the couch. Twice, she went over to the bottom of the stairs, looked up and seemed to decide that they were too much to take on. Normally, after a nice feed, she liked nothing more than to go upstairs to sleep.

At ten minutes to six, Olwen lifted her up and put her in the back seat of the car. It is a fifteen-minute drive into Carrick. I drove slowly but, as we turned a bend, a car came out from a side road and I had to brake hard. Pepe fell off the seat. I knew she would not be able to get back up on her own, so I had to pull the car in and Olwen got out, opened the back door and put her back up on the seat. As always, Pepe did not complain. It was a lovely, ironic, pathetic moment. Settling her down, making her comfortable, before she died.

We drove into the backyard of the vet's. Olwen went into the clinic to tell them that we had arrived. The surgery was very busy. It was at least ten minutes before Olwen got to see the vet. She explained that the car was unlocked and that Pepe was asleep there, and that she and I would be in the café across the road. She gave the vet her mobile number. The vet agreed that she would go out and give Pepe the injection. When it was all over, and she had taken her from the car, she would text Olwen.

I did not want to open the back door in case it would wake Pepe, so I leaned over and talked to her for the last time. I am not sure if she heard anything. I think she raised her head for a moment. But the occasion was getting to me. It was like being at the edge of a diving board. Eventually, with tears streaming down my face, I said goodbye. I closed the car door quietly and went across the road to the café.

I hope that she died peacefully. I remonstrate with myself: I should not have been selfish, I should have stayed with her and held and cuddled her as the medication took effect. How could I have left her to die alone? What if the injection did not work? What if she awoke and was distressed?

There were, on reflection, many reasons why I could not bring myself to be with her as she died. The main one was that I was afraid it would unleash the memory of the last moments with Aileen. It was also – and I had forgotten about this until Olwen reminded me – because when it came to the time of Frodo being given his lethal injection, I hugged and talked to Frodo before the vet came in and, after the injection was given, bawled my heart out.

There was also the memory of Luke, of that moment when Aileen and I went in to the intensive-care room to say goodbye and it was impossible to hold and kiss him as his little body was full of wires and tubes keeping him alive.

I grew up in a Catholic culture in which a 'good' death was revered. I never found out what exactly a good death was, but I think it had to do with being fully conscious, enveloped in prayer and, despite whatever pain was being suffered, being willing to embrace it. Since Christ died the ultimate good death, on the cross for our sins, the task for us Christians was to emulate him.

But wouldn't it be lovely to slip away like Pepe? Unsuspectingly falling asleep on the back seat of the car, perhaps thinking she was on her way to Dublin. In the middle of the afternoon, on the road to nowhere, she quietly stopped being.

The Sense of Loss

For a long time before, but increasingly as I began to contemplate Pepe's end, I worried about how I would deal with the grief. It is the most excruciating of emotions, so intense, so unpredictable, so personal. It is love turned inside out. You go on loving, but the object of your love is no longer there. All those days of thinking, worrying and caring suddenly come to an end. She is gone but she is present, everywhere. And yet there is an emptiness. All the signs of life – her bed, her food dishes, her lead – become signs of death. She presides in her absence.

Doing my exercises on the mornings after her death, there was no sensation of her sniffing and licking my toes as I stretched out to reach them, and there never would be again. Worst of all is the absence of the welcome I got when I came home, or down to the kitchen in the morning. The sheer exuberance, the joy of being alive, the energy that she created, the excitement, the pleasure of being together, the hopes and joys of what the day might bring. All gone.

That night, Carol, Olwen and I sat around, drinking wine, sharing memories of Pepe, recounting her antics and misdemeanours. It was a mixture of laughter and sadness. It was a ritual way of dealing with death.

It was a private affair. It did not occur to me to phone or text anyone or put a message on the family app. Many of the stories we told revolved around Aileen and the relationship between her and Pepe. It was a way of remembering them both. Often when Olwen came home from school and Aileen and I were at work, she would allow Pepe up to the living room and sit with her while watching television. If she heard Aileen's car pulling up outside, she would have to grab Pepe and bring her downstairs to the kitchen before Aileen came in. When Pepe was a pup, Olwen would always back me up when it came to defending food being stolen, table and chair legs gnawed, or clothes destroyed. During Aileen's illness and after her death, Pepe became the bond that held Olwen and me together. Olwen was only thirteen when Aileen was first diagnosed with cancer. She was sixteen when she died. At one point in our memorialising, Olwen stopped and said, 'You know, I spent more years with Pepe than I did with Aileen.'

Olwen and I talked about Aileen in a way that we had not done before. For many years after Aileen died, I found it very difficult to talk about her or look at a photo of her without breaking into tears. The consequence was that Arron and Olwen found it difficult to talk with me about her because they felt it made me sad. It wasn't a complete silence. We always remembered her. We held parties to celebrate her. There were photos of her throughout the house. I looked at them, but it was always painful. I wrote about her, and that was also a struggle. But talking was particularly difficult. Olwen was great at telling stories about Aileen, laughing about her foibles and the ways she related to Pepe. I smiled but found it hard to laugh.

The next morning, Olwen went back to Dublin, and Carol and I went for a walk in Lough Key Forest Park. It was one of Pepe's favourite places, and it is a place where doggy people go. I should have realised it would be an emotional minefield. I was walking slowly because I had hurt my Achilles tendon.

Soon after the walk began, I was approached by a whippet, one of the friendliest of dogs. I bent down to pet her and I could not prevent the tears welling up. I told the owner about my loss. She laid her hand on my shoulder, and the whippet gave me a lick.

It was a beautiful spring day, with the sun streaming through the soft green filigree of the new leaves, lighting up the lichens and mosses on the trees. Of all the pleasures of being with Pepe, there were few as good as witnessing her excitement at being out in the countryside, off the lead, free to run and explore the world. I have an image of her bouncing up and down through the purple heather that covers the mountains in autumn, looking out for me, trying to find a path. And I can see her in Cruagh woods in the Dublin mountains and the joy in her face as she comes running through the undergrowth in the pine forests, with a stick that she thinks is perfect for throwing, her hair matted with burrs and needles, her paws and legs covered in mud.

As we turned on to one of the main paths of the forest park, I saw in the distance two water spaniels coming towards us with their owners. I knew that they would soon catch up with us. And yet it was a surprise when I felt one of them right behind me. I turned and bent down to pet it. It did not move. The owners caught up and the woman said to me: 'Wow, that is very strange, she is normally so shy,' and walked on. And I wondered, as I walked away, if the dog had sensed my grief.

As we got back to where we had parked the car, we encountered a woman starting out on her own walk. She had two dogs, one more friendly than the other. I asked the woman: 'Where would we be without dogs?' She replied simply: 'We'd be lost,' and then she said: 'Wouldn't the world be a better place if there were more dogs and less humans.'

The Work of Pepe

Pepe helped me be compassionate. I realise that not all dogs succeed in this work: Blondi didn't prevent Hitler from being a monster. But there were many times when I felt that Pepe helped me to be more compassionate, to be more aware of my being in the world.

There were so many times when she would come up to me and do nothing but stand silently beside me. It was as if she needed to be refuelled by my presence. I would stop what I was doing, reading, writing or watching television, and gaze into her eyes. During these moments, there was a sense of us being caught in time, she as a dog, me as a human, and that all that we had for each other was a sense of being together. Staring into her eyes was like staring into eternity. In those moments, I was often overwhelmed by a sense of the unpredictability and futility of life, of our attempts to cre- ate some centre, some meaning that we can hold on to, that binds us together. Something whereby two could become one. And I would feel for her, not because she was in any distress, but because she was doing all that she could, as a dog, to reach out across the divide and be with me.

The German philosopher Arthur Schopenhauer was very fond of dogs, particularly his two poodles. As he grew older, he became increasingly pessimistic about the possibility of sustaining fulfilling relations with other human beings and began to spend more time with his dogs. He praised the 'moral and intellectual qualities of dogs' and said that 'anyone who has never owned a dog can't know what loving and being loved mean.'

Mourning Rituals

What makes the loss of a dog different from the loss of another loved one is that there is no mechanism for attaining sympathy and support. No announcement in the paper, no funeral, no wearing of black, no collective mourning. For a while, I thought of walking around the streets of Carrick and the paths of Lough Key with Pepe's lead dangling from my hand. Maybe I should have held some kind of ceremony and invited my dog-loving friends to share memories of her.

The absence of mourning rituals for dogs is strange. Many people love their dogs. When their dogs die, many suffer an intense sense of loss. But there are not the same ways of recognising the loss, of talking about it, of letting people know the grief that is being experienced. It becomes internalised.

It is as if there is some unwritten rule that says that while it is all right to love your dog when it is alive, when it dies, it is not all right to go into mourning in the way people do when a human loved one dies. And yet the loss of a dog can, for many people, be akin to losing a father, mother, wife, husband, daughter or son. When love is denied, it can become a source of shame and embarrassment. When we cannot declare our love, when it is suppressed or, worse still, deliberately repressed, we are forced to live a lie.

There are ways of remembering a dead dog. You can talk about it, but only in a certain way and only for a certain length of time. If you talk too often or too much, even with family, friends and neighbours, there is a danger of not just losing sympathy but of being considered a bit odd. When Aileen and Luke died, I often cried in public and I did not feel embarrassed or ashamed. I am not so sure it would have been the same if I had cried about Pepe.

The absence of rituals and public recognition around the loss of a dog, or any pet, needs to be addressed. I know people who have photos of their dead dog, or dogs, at home, but I have never seen one on an office desk. I am not aware of anyone who has asked for or been granted compassionate leave when their dog dies. I know of nobody who celebrates their dead dog's anniversary. And although it was popular among Victorians, I know of nobody who has got their dead dog stuffed.

I am not suggesting that we should have funerals for pets, but maybe some kind of gathering, some ritual to help mend the emotional wounds. Given that you can get a card for almost anything these days, from passing an exam to passing a driving test, it is remarkable that commercial card companies have not exploited the dead-dog market.

It may be that social media is bridging the gap. The day after Pepe died, I learned that Cuss, my good friend in Canada, had Meb, his Brittany spaniel, put to sleep a week before Pepe died. He told me that his wife, Mary, had put a post on Facebook and the response had been phenomenal. He wrote:

We were stunned by the amount and variety of replies. I never knew that people took dogs so seriously and we had about 30 posts that were all empathetic and concerned. And then that Saturday on the hike, Brian stopped in the middle of the woods and asked me to say a few words . . . Meb grew up on the hikes – went on her first aged 6 months and in her prime went on 3 a week and ran her legs off. I had always said that when she could no longer hike, her life would have no meaning and that I would put her down. But even though she could no longer hike we kept her going for another two years. On the hike I just said that 'Meb's dead', and then as we all used to do, asked them to call after her. So it was quite the sound – 40 adults in the woods laughing and shouting, 'Meb, Meb.'

Love Never Dies

Grief is an exquisite pain. The one you have loved is gone. When Aileen died, part of me died. It felt as if a vital organ had been taken out of my being. Aileen still presides in her absence, but not as intensely as she did for the first few years after her death. Time heals. Other things and people begin to fill the void.

Pepe still presides throughout the house, in the car and in the garden. But her smell is beginning to fade. I take the rug from the living room and wash it with a power hose. I gather up her turds from the lawn. I put her beds in the bin. I gather together all the tins of dog food, the biscuits and dental sticks, and put them in a bag for Donal's Duckie. It is all done in a matter of hours. It took me five years before I could clear out Aileen's wardrobe.

The Sunday after Pepe's death day, I awoke and looked out over the lake. The mist was beginning to lift. It was going to be a fine day. I needed to immerse myself in it. After Aileen died, I learned the importance of keeping going, of thrashing through the water of life to stop from drowning. I regularly disappeared on my bike into the Wicklow hills. And in the days after Pepe died, I took to the lanes and byways of Roscommon and Sligo, of Lough Arrow and Lough Key.

Another survival tactic after Aileen died was to talk and talk about her, about the last week, the last day, the last few hours. It was as if the more I told the story to different people, the more I would understand it. But the problem was that when I talked, I would often cry. Bringing back those memories was too painful. I would try to hold back the tears, but then the dam would burst. I can imagine how difficult it must have been for family and friends to listen to and bear with me, but many did. It took me years to realise that while almost everyone else had moved on, I was still stuck in the mud. I could no longer tell the story.

I had feared that when Pepe died, I would be once again overwhelmed with grief. But no: I could think of her without crying. Tears would well up, but the dam did not burst. It was more of a numb sensation. I could talk and write about her without crying.

The Sunday after Pepe died, as I descended down from Fox Hill into Cootehall, I realised that it was Mass time. It is the only time of the week that Cootehall is busy. As I passed by, I saw my neighbour Anne. I felt the need to stop and tell her the news of Pepe's demise. I wanted to tell the whole world, but I made do with telling Anne. She is a doggy woman. She walks Roxy up and down the road past my house. He is a lovely dog, as friendly as Anne. But, from the beginning, for some reason only understood by herself, Pepe could not stand him. I often wanted to invite Anne in for a cup of tea. But I couldn't.

Anne was doing a church-gate collection with a man I did not know. There were still fifteen minutes before Mass would begin and so I did not feel I was taking up their time. I apologised to the man and said that I had to stop and tell Anne, and she told me that there was no need to apologise, as he was a doggy man as well. So I briefly told the story of the last few days, the planning of Pepe's death, how Olwen had come down from Dublin and how it had all gone alphabetically.

As I cycled away, I realised that I would not be able to share my grief with other people from the neighbourhood. This was my own fault. I had not found a way of integrating into the community. I do not go to Mass. I don't have children in the local school. I don't go to GAA matches and I only rarely go to the pub.

Many people get a dog immediately after their previous one has died. Some even get another dog prior to the older dog dying. Presumably it eases the transition. But others go through a period of grief that prevents forming a new relationship. I am one of those. Shortly after Pepe died, someone asked me if I would be getting another dog soon. It was a simple question and, among doggy people, often asked. But I was hurt. I felt like saying that, when Aileen died, nobody asked me the following week if I would be getting another woman. It was not that I thought that I would never have a relationship with someone after Aileen died. It was more that I wanted to grieve fully. I had loved and lived with Aileen for thirty-seven years. I wanted to let go of her gently. I was afraid of my grief being contaminated. What woman would tolerate me ranting on about the love I had for Aileen?

It is nothing like this with Pepe. I loved her very much and I miss her in many different ways. But there is not the same rich, thick, complex relationship with a dog. I did realise myself through Pepe; she became a mirror through which I understood myself and what it is to live life. But it is nothing at all like the love I had for Aileen.

In the case of Pepe, it is also about being free again: no longer having to be attuned to her needs and interests, or worrying about her. I can come and go as I please. I can go to Dublin, or on holidays, without having to make complex arrangements for her care. A new dog is a commitment I am reluctant to make. A dog is for life, but if I got a new one, particularly a puppy, I would be odds on to die first.

And yet there is this strong pull to experience new life. To develop a relationship. To go out and explore together. To marvel at the way she sees, smells and understands the world. A world of magic and excitement. To be mesmerised by her antics. To be warmed by her affection and trust. To sympathise with her when she is hurt or afraid. To love and care for her.

Acknowledgements

I would not have written this book without the encouragement of David Blake Knox. When he was writing his *The Curious History of Irish Dogs*, we talked a lot about our relationship with our dogs. He suggested that I write something about my relationship with Pepe. I did. It has become the opening section of the book. Sometime later, when I described how I was trying to explore new forms of writing, he told me to write about Pepe.

This is not an academic book. I have been informed and inspired by a wide range of scientific books and articles about dogs and other pets, as well as many novels, memoirs and short stories. One of the best novels describing the relationship between humans and their dogs is Sara Baume's *spill simmer falter wither*. She captures the commitment of a marginalised elderly man who takes on a rescue dog that continually causes him anguish, shame and grief. J. R. Ackerley's *My Dog Tulip* has rightly come to be seen as a classic. It is a wacky and endearing story of a lonely, literate man taking on a dog and his developing love and commitment to her. Similarly, I was taken by Eileen Battersby's *Ordinary Dogs* and her descriptions of the adventures, joy and happiness that her dogs brought her.

This is a love story, and I have come to realise that as much as there is a genre of fiction that describes romantic love, there is a growing market for dog-lit books, as well of course as the numerous films and television programmes. This is all because in the last couple of hundred years, dogs, as well as cats and other pets, have become such important objects of love for humans. Many scientists have sought to understand the relationship between dogs and humans. Alexandra Horowitz has written three bestselling books in which she mixes the personal with the scientific: *Inside of a Dog: What Dogs See, Smell and Know*; *Being a Dog: Following the Dog into a World of Smell* and, more recently, *Our Dogs, Ourselves: The Story of a Singular Bond*.

Among those who have explored the history of dogs and other pets, I have relied on Konrad Lorenz's *Man Meets Dog*; Keith Thomas's *Man and the Natural World: A History of Modern Sensibility*; Yi-Fu Tuan's *Dominance and Affection: The Making of Pets*; Katharine Rogers's *First Friend: A History of Dogs and Humans*; Katherine Grier's *Pets in America: A History*; Susan McHugh's *Dog*; Kathleen Kete's *The Beast in the Boudoir: Petkeeping in Nineteenth-century Paris*; Alan Beck and Aaron Katcher's *Pets and People: The Importance of Animal Companionship*; Laura Brown's *Fables of Modernity: Literature and Culture in the English Eighteenth Century*; Raymond Pierotti and Brandy Fogg's *The First Domestication: How Wolves and*

Humans Coevolved; Rhoda Lerman's *In the Company of New-fies*; Jacky Colliss Harvey's *The Animal's Companion: People and Their Pets, a 26,000-year-old Love Story*; James Serpell's *In the Company of Animals: A Study of Human–Animal Relationships*; Margo DeMello's *Animals and Society: An Introduction to Human–Animal Studies*; Harriet Ritvo's *The Animal Estate: The English and Other Creatures in the Victorian Age*; Adrian Franklin's *Animals and Modern Cultures: A Sociology of Human–Animal Relations in Modernity*; Ingrid Tague's *Animal Companions: Pets and Social Change in Eighteenth-century Britain* and Donna Haraway's *The Companion Species Manifesto: Dogs, People, and Significant Otherness*.

Academic articles consulted include John Archer's 'Why Do People Love Their Pets?'; Leslie Irvine's 'Pampered or Enslaved? The Moral Dilemmas of Pets'; Lawrence Kurdek's 'Pet Dogs as Attachment Figures for Adult Owners' and 'Pet Dogs as Attachment Figures'; Charles Phineas's 'Household Pets and Urban Alienation'; Clinton Sanders's 'Actions Speak Louder than Words: Close Relationships between Humans and Nonhuman Animals'; Froma Walsh's 'Human–Animal Bonds 1: The Relational Significance of Companion Animals'; Hal Herzog's 'Why People Care More about Pets than Other Humans'; Sigal Zilcha-Mano, Mario Mikulincer and Phillip Shaver's 'An Attachment Perspective on Human–Pet Relationships'; Marc Shell's 'The Family Pet'; Bridget Waller et al's 'Paedomorphic Facial Expressions Give Dogs a Selective Advantage'; David Peña-Guzmán's

'Can Nonhuman Animals Commit Suicide?' and, perhaps the best-titled article, Monique Udell and C. Wynne's 'A Review of Domestic Dogs' (*Canis familiaris*) Human-Like Behaviors: or Why Behavior Analysts Should Stop Worrying and Love Their Dogs'.

There are myriad facts and figures about dogs and other pets. The ones that I have cited in this book are taken from reliable sources, but they may differ from other equally good sources. They should be seen as indicative rather than as scientifically accurate. The stories that I have taken from newspapers are, I hope, factual.

As always, my friend Michael Cussen (Cuss) has been enormously encouraging and supportive not just in reading an earlier draft but in helping me understand life with and without dogs. Avril Burgess was insightful and rigorous in her comments.

I had heard that Brendan Barrington in Penguin was probably the best editor in Ireland. Having worked with him, I can fully support this. His ability to take charge of the text – to see all its strengths and weaknesses, to draw out the best from what I wrote, to linger over a couple of lines or paragraph and sniff out their essence, and to bravely prune what he thought irrelevant – was amazing.

My daughter, Olwen, read an earlier draft and reminded me of stories about Pepe. Talking about Pepe got us through some very tough times. As always in recent years, Carol MacKeogh was my first reader, my best critic and my most ardent supporter.